NEW
NATIVE
AMERICAN
DRAMA

NEW
NATIVE AMERICAN
DRAMA

University of Oklahoma Press   Norman and London

THREE PLAYS

by Hanay Geiogamah

Introduction by Jeffrey Huntsman

Library of Congress Cataloging in Publication Data

Geiogamah, Hanay, 1945–
    New Native American drama.

    CONTENTS: Body Indian.—Foghorn.—49.
    1. Indians of North America—Drama.   I.   Title.
PS3557.E357N4   812′.54   79–4733
ISBN: 0–8061–1697–8

5   6   7   8   9   10   11   12   13   14   15   16   17   18

FOR ELLEN STEWART
OF LA MAMA E.T.C.

Contents

Introduction

BY JEFFREY HUNTSMAN

THE PLAYS in this volume are exciting instances of an art form that is at once ancient and modern. As the first plays published by a Native American, Hanay Geiogamah's dramas represent a newly emerging theatrical impulse from a group of Americans who have already found moving artistic expression in song, poetry, prose, painting, and sculpture. These plays grew out of their author's desire to present Native Americans to Native Americans in ways that are vivid and compelling and free from the more pernicious of the Euro-American stereotypes of Indians. Because he writes about them with the understanding of an intimate, Geiogamah's Indians are neither the noble savages of Ann J. Kemble Hatton's *Tammany* (1794) nor the vicious subhumans of Joseph McCoy's *Frontier Maid* (1819); nor are they the caricatures patronized by contemporary cinema in performances by Sal Mineo, Jeff Chandler, or even Jay Silverheels and Dan George. They are instead his neighbors, his family and friends, himself—people who in the past were perhaps forced to suffer the injustices of the dominant Anglo society but who now can again comprehend and mold their own lives. To speak to his people in an aesthetically powerful way, Hanay Geiogamah turned to a European literary form that was new to Indian artists.

Yet, although these particular plays are new and represent a new art form for Native Americans, the essential theatrical impulse is an ancient one. Literature, in its broadest and most profound sense, includes all purposeful and perennial art in language. The *Iliad*, the *Bhagavad Gita*, and *Beowulf* were literature long before they were *litterae*, and so were the tales of the Anishinabes, the songs of the Kwakiutls, and the chantways of the Navajos. Until very recently, however, traditional Indian literature has been badly presented to English-speaking audiences. In thin, unpalatable translations, removed from its dramatic context of performance—where dance, music, and literary text are intricately bound together—it seems poor, dead stuff. Stripped of the rhythms of singer and dancer, of the subtle gestures of men and women experienced in transmitting the wisdom of their nation, such literature often appears unappealing and unmoving, a set of emotionally flat cultural artifacts wanting humanity the way an elk's-tooth dress or an eagle dancer's costume in a museum case wants an animating human body. And these dimensions of the complete literary experience are not—however much the outward trappings may have altered—the vanished things of the Vanishing American, found only in scholars' reconstructions. They have lived in the memories of active people and, allowing for the changes inevitable in all such living traditions, are still alive today.

It is perhaps this continuity, however altered and redefined, that accounts in part for the relative lateness with which Native Americans have turned to drama as a literary form; their inclination to theatricality, performance, and, most importantly, participation in a shared event has continued to be satisfied by enduring religious practices, powwows, and even the 49s that furnish the setting for the third play in this volume. It is partly this sense of participation and continuity with a remembered or imagined past that makes Geiogamah's plays so successful in the theater, especially with Indian audiences. But most of all, these plays are excellent drama, performances that entertain and instruct in the best traditions of both Indians and Europeans and that speak to Indian audiences in ways that much other literature has not.

Geiogamah's interest does not lie in reconstructing the dear, dead, romanticized past when every phrase had a poetic sparkle and every utterance was an oration. Nor does it lie in a self-indulgent vituperation of the White Man and his forked culture, where the failures of 1978 are blamed on the slaughter of the buffalo a century before. His purpose is, first, to present and thereby preserve *living* Indian traditions and, next, to demonstrate the facts of Indian life in America today, unvarnished by either Indian or non-Indian romanticizers. Comparisons with the black theater of the 1960s, made by several reviewers across the country, are simply not apt. In its political aspect Geiogamah's call is not Baraka's shout for mayhem and revolution; it is rather the alarm of Thoreau's Chanticleer (or the warning blast of a foghorn), designed to stimulate Indian people to think about their lives of quiet or confirmed desperation. Consequently, he is interested more in survival and self-knowledge than in reproach and confrontation. While the plays contain many images of past injustices—like the iconic buffalo skeletons in *49*—their function is to emphasize the contemporary result, not the historical and reprehensible cause. His intention is political in the broadest sense of that word; these plays are not only the self-expressions of the artist but also his deliberate messages to a community, urging its members to note their condition, whether it arises from external prejudice (as in *Foghorn*) or from Indians' mistreatment of one other (as in *Body Indian*). It is not surprising that the results of murder, exploitation, misappropriation, and prejudice are represented in these plays, for such things loom large in recent Indian history. But they are the givens, the facts of the social and political environment in which Native Americans live today. When Geiogamah presents a stereotype, as he does throughout *Foghorn*, it is to provide his audience an occasion to exorcise their own acceptance of the ancestral noble savage—dour, stoic, and dumb—or the contemporary welfare derelict—drunken, irresponsible, and shiftless. This purpose he accomplishes with unflagging good humor, classically exposing absurdity with teasing caricature.

It is, in fact, just this emphasis on what *is* and on the process of maintaining a sense of community and continuity that ties both the essential form and the intention of Hanay Geiogamah's plays to ancient Indian practices. Nearly every important group effort for Native Americans was religious in some basic sense, and Native American religious ceremonies are basically dramatic. Unlike the religious ceremonies typical of the Judeo-Christian experience, which chiefly seek to invoke a future benefit or to celebrate a past one, most Native American ceremonies assert a present truth—the Sun Dance lodge *is* the center of the universe; the Katchinas *are* the powers of the universe; the Navajo chantways *do* recreate a portion of the universe. In the same way, these plays take the ongoing process of creation both as their chief philosophical theme and as their central organizing principle. As Singing Man in *49* says, "I know many songs which are not finished. They are still songs." There may come a time when true peace and understanding exists, "when a man will not hurt a man by killing his way of living"; until then Indian peoples must stand together.

The plays printed in this volume were all premiered by the Native American Theater Ensemble (NATE, earlier known as the American Indian Theater Ensemble), a troupe Geiogamah organized in 1972 with the help of Ellen Stewart, director and wizard-in-residence of La Mama Experimental Theater Club in New York City. Ms. Stewart, with her legendary skill and energy, helped obtain grants for the company from the National Endowment for the Arts and the Ford and Rockefeller foundations. Beginning with a list of some two hundred names, Geiogamah selected about sixty talented Indian artists, from which the company of sixteen was assembled, a unique ethnic-theater group drawn from and directed toward Native Americans. In the fall of 1972 the ensemble opened in New York with Geiogamah's *Body Indian*. The company later toured throughout the United States, performing at the Smithsonian Museum in Washington, D.C., and in Oklahoma,

Colorado, New Mexico, Arizona, Washington, California, Wisconsin, and Illinois—and even played for six weeks at the Reichskabaret in Berlin. Everywhere their reception by critics was sympathetic and generally good, even if the reviews often revealed the critics to be puzzled by the plays and ignorant of Indian traditions, values, and aesthetics. Whatever their critical insights, however, critics and audiences alike seemed to agree with Clive Barnes of the *New York Times* that the inaugural performance marked "the birth of an interesting and fresh theatrical project."

Body Indian, NATE's premiere production, is a startling, disturbing, but ultimately triumphant play. Breaking with the romanticized tradition of earlier stage Indians, it opens in a cheerless, dingy apartment, where four people are asleep or collapsed from several days of continual drinking. Bobby Lee—crippled by the loss of a leg, unsteady because of his handicap and too much alcohol, and painfully seeking the sociability and reassurance of his friends—struggles up the stairs to the apartment. He brings with him two relatives, several bottles of cheap wine, and an acute need for companionship and affection. As the characters continue to drink, they talk about the superficial but revealing concerns of the moment—especially the perpetual shortage of money and the growing threat of running out of booze. Bobby has just leased his allotment of land and wants to enter a six-week rehabilitation program for alcoholics. Significantly, he intends to pay the four-hundred-dollar fee for the treatment, although he could have it free; whatever the cause of his drinking, he is a man of character and decency. Representing an impulse toward self-help and dignity, Bobby wants to solve his problems by his own efforts and with his own money. Unfortunately, his friends and relatives are too inundated by their own selfish interests to cooperate or even acquiesce. The first scene, like the four that follow, ends as Bobby passes out and his friends solicitously roll him for his money—ostensibly to buy more wine for the party but actually to hide it away for the time when both liquor and money run out and each person, they feel, must fend alone.

On the surface the play is about the devastating effects of alcohol and the stresses of modern society. But more importantly, it is about the way people—Indian people in particular—abuse, degrade, and cripple each other and themselves, effects they can have only because they are intimately and ineluctably involved with each other. As the play progresses, one realizes that the community in Howard's grubby room is both example and exemplar of the Indian world at large, the maimed but still vital body politic. The people in *Body Indian* are members of several different tribes (a fact not stressed in the text but immediately obvious to Indian audiences), and the world of the stage is a microcosm, an allegory of Indian life. From the opening image of Bobby's halting progress up the stairs, the play develops almost ritualistically, manifesting the dark forces of a troubled society, covertly at first, in empty solicitude and forced camaraderie, and later in open and unalloyed badness. In their weakness and inveterate misery, the thieves know they do wrong, yet they half-convince themselves that their hell is inevitable and that their only recourse is surrender. So, rather than support Bobby in his resolve for salvation, they undermine him and weaken themselves.

The five scenes of the play are essentially identical in their internal arrangement: after much drink and conversation Bobby passes out and is robbed of some of the money he intended for his treatment. Each scene ends with the passing of a train, whose rumble, whistle, and lights overwhelm the action and, mixed with the sounds of drums and dance rattles, freeze it momentarily as the characters ponder the import of their actions. For each character in turn the train is eidetic—for all but Bobby a persistent reminder of their guilt and for Bobby in the final moment of the play a brutal and appallingly vivid re-creation of the accident that cost him a leg. Yet for all their similarities, the scenes are not repetitive. The first establishes the pattern of actions and relationships; the second, slow and measured, focuses on the men and their alcoholic escape from some kind of unexpressed moral improbity, cheerlessness, and misery. The third scene is the women's, whose drinking is, in an odd sense, somewhat more positive—a lively convention for mutual support that has evolved out of a life of drudgery, too many children, and money insufficient at times even for subsistence. The youths dominate the fourth scene with their friendly engagement and energy. Yet, although they are quick, bright, and vital, they are compelled by the same deprivations that compelled their parents—lack of money, an unacknowledged hopelessness bordering on desperation, and a moral dislocation—into pointless, frenetic, and shallow pursuits, and they are as quick as their elders to take advantage of Bobby. Throughout, the intensity of the action, the oppression of the train's dominating presence, and the seriousness of the thievery increase inexorably. At the end Bobby's friends are wholly engulfed by their most self-deceptive rationalization. Where Alice had earlier asked, with a familial solicitude tinged with self-interest, "Does my nephew have any more money?" now Howard spins an elaborate excuse for stealing more of Bobby's money: he does it in order to buy more wine so that Bobby won't have to suffer the DTs when he awakens. When they can find no money, they take Bobby's artificial leg to be pawned, a mean and brutal act, adding disfigurement to his handicap. The play ends as all the strands of the action come together. Bobby discovers that his leg is missing and sardonically parodies the opening line: "Welll, Helllooo, Bobby Lee. How are you, hites? Long time no . . . seeeee." Then he is overcome by the horror of it all, and he sees again the train bearing down on him, mangling his leg, as the sound and light recapitulate each of the earlier scenes.

Body Indian is tough, gritty, and powerful. Despite their elements of decency and pride, Geiogamah's characters rend each other, sometimes exultantly, sometimes apologetically, but always in ways that ultimately point to truth. This truth is often humorous, presented with a directness that is characteristic of Indians when they talk among themselves. When the women speak about their perennial lack of money, Bobby says:

Every Indian needs to have a government check for $25,000. They could give you womens $50 thousand. Then you could buy all your kids shoes, clothes, bicycles, pay rent, pay fines, buy shawls and earrings, and put the money you have left in the bank to live on. That's the only way you'd ever have the money you need.

They all laugh, but the truth cuts: the significant poverty is not the one that results from the temporary absence of money (although that is cruel and real enough); it is rather the one that comes from the sense of perpetual misery and disjunction and produces unhappiness and treachery among friends and relatives. The laughter that greets Bobby's remark is typically Indian—sometimes uneasy and bitter but always revealing: it helps maintain the social equilibrium, for those things that are in the open, subject to teasing and even ridicule, cannot fester and breed unconscious discontent. Howard's militant but empty jibe at the police is countered by Ethel's "Are you going to do a war dance for us?" which good-naturedly joshes Howard about his age and lack of energy but which also sets his remark in its proper political perspective. Even the lighter moments are turned subtly to significance. Bobby's jailhouse apparition of multicolored chickens singing Indian songs— disturbingly resonant of a religious vision—is an absurdly funny example of the DTs, a condition to be avoided whatever its occasional moments of retrospective levity. Throughout *Body Indian*, Geiogamah's humor tempers his message. However grim and powerful its thrust, Indian audiences find the play funny, as Geiogamah intended it to be, for Indian people have always known that in humor is truth and that truth is always best presented with the perspective that humor provides. Because he speaks with honesty and humor and because he is himself an Indian, Geiogamah can speak directly, without preaching or finger-wagging, in a manner that would mark impertinence or temerity in a non-Indian. *Body Indian* is in fact a play with a purpose. When Bobby reaches out for sanity and salvation, his people evade him, partly in order to satisfy their more superficial needs but partly to avoid a kind of frighteningly profound contact with each other. Geiogamah's message is clear: if Indian people are to survive with a measure of decency and dignity, they must stick together. Yet, although Bobby's final cry of anguish is a denunciation of what has happened to him, it is directed not toward his friends but toward his own trust in people too weak and pliable to give him the support he sought. In suffering injustice at their hands, Bobby has also profited. His suffering has been redemptive, and this realization ultimately makes *Body Indian* a play of optimism and triumph.

Geiogamah's second play, *Foghorn*, is perhaps the most immediately accessible of the three. It premiered in Berlin—an appropriate happenstance for this outrageous Brechtian confrontation with Indian stereotypes ranging in time from Columbus to the 1973 incident at Wounded Knee. The title refers to the harassing foghorns set to blast continually at the Indians who occupied Alcatraz in 1969, but metaphorically it represents the playwright's awakening call to Indian people about the dangers that stereotypes pose. For such images limit the humanity not only of their originators, the non-Indians who invented such roles as the noble savage, the thieving redskin, the shy princess, but also of Indians themselves, who often find that they are living down to others' expectations. Technically the play is a modern, multimedia extravaganza with music, lights, graphics, and human actors, and there is a gentle irony in using such elements in juxtaposition to the traditional clothing and material possessions of earlier times. As in his other plays, however,

Geiogamah is not particularly interested in castigating the Euro-Americans for past injustices. Rather, he seeks to present these stereotypes in a new light, twisting them into new configurations and helping audiences exorcise them with knowledgeable laughter. Even if it is viewed merely as a set of loosely connected skits, much like a minstrel show in a different color, the play is very funny and very effective. Some of the elements border on slapstick: the list of broken treaties written on toilet paper; the Roman Catholic nun with a cross, not even of gold, but of paper money, whose "holy book" is the yellow pages. Other portions are broadly parodic: the Watergate-tinged spy who uses the Nixon slush fund to buy off the Indians who are occupying the Bureau of Indian Affairs headquarters in Washington; the sly Pocahontas coyly describing Captain Smith's sudden impotence; the caricature of Lady Bird Johnson redesignating an Indian reservation as a national park, because Indians "get very little use of them anyway."

The most effective parts of the play, however, are more subtle—matters of structure, dialogue, and diction. Separate events, simply funny in isolation, are tellingly connected for an ultimately greater effect. The landing of Columbus demands to be compared with the landing of Native Americans on Alcatraz; the United States senator's speech, where Native Americans are given reservations that "we have generously set aside for them," contrasts ironically with the Alcatraz declaration that promises the majority inhabitants of this country "a portion of the land for their own, to be held in trust by the American Indian people—for as long as the sun shall rise and the rivers go down to the sea"; and the hysterical schoolmarm's obsession with white civilization—"The English language that has brought hope and civilization to people everywhere. . . . The American way begins with hello"—appears ludicrous next to the Alcatraz statement:

We will further guide the majority inhabitants in the proper way of living. We will offer them our religion, our education, our way of life—in order to help them achieve our level of civilization and thus raise them and all their white brothers from their savage and unhappy state.

Geiogamah constantly mocks the diction of both the Indian-haters ("a wild mob of hot-blooded savages," "squaws and bucks," "Indians that American people can be proud of, not shamed by") and the romanticizing Indian-lovers ("beautiful costumes," "miserable and poor and our most isolated minor-ity," "vanishing specimens of primitive mankind," "colorful native"). The wishy-washy liberal gets a proper dose, too, when the First Lady gushes over the "lovely stoic faces" and the Lone Ranger suggests that he could take the wounded Tonto "to a friendly rancher's house, one where they'll let me bring my Injun friend inside."

As the play progresses, the humor becomes more pointed as a ridiculous Wild West Show enactment of "A Savage, Brutal Scalp Dance" merges into the murder of a drummer at Wounded Knee. The play ends much as it began, with the parade of the arrested occupiers of Wounded Knee paralleling the march of the nineteenth-century victims of the Trail of Tears, and with the Narrator, speaking both for the defendants in the Wounded Knee courtroom and for all Indian people, crying, "I am NOT GUILTY!" His words come immediately upon the reprise of the opening, a Spanish sailor committing the first crime against Native Americans by mistaking them for Asians: "Ellos son los indios!" The repetition focuses the play's tricky irony: Native Americans are not guilty of the misconceptions in others' minds, nor of the behavior encoded in assaultive or paternalistic white stereotypes, nor of the things for which Indians have suffered injustice, inhumanity, and brutality. Such practices are degrading to all of us, irrespective of whether we perpetuate them actively or allow them to continue by acquiescing in their use. As in all of his drama, Geiogamah asks first that we study and understand ourselves and then make responsible and humane use of that knowledge.

The third and latest play of the set, *49*, is the most theatrically sophisticated and the most direct of Geiogamah's plays. At the same time, although conventionally European in its structure, *49* can be called the most traditionally Native American of the three, both in the way it centers on the maintenance of an eternal *now* and in the way it uses the elements of dance and music—movement and mime, songs and whistles, flutes, bells, and drums. The play's traditional dances of people and animals are mimetic, and so are the actors' imitations of things like automobiles. The opening of scene 4, when the gathering gradually emerges from a slow assemblage of the sounds of people, dance bells, flutes, and drums, is a theatrical event of considerable grace.

49 is a splendidly balanced blend of a contemporary social event, the 49, with elements of a traditional past and a forward-looking shamanistic vision. A 49 is a time when Indian people, mostly young, gather for a night of singing, dancing, and conversation, predictably leavened, like most parties everywhere, by the promise of intoxicants and sex. The point of the 49 is not chiefly that it is Bacchanalian but that it is a chosen time for meeting and enjoyment, for a renewing of strength and identity. Since they generally take place in the countryside, 49s, no matter how raucous they may become, are socially less deleterious than a boisterous night in a city bar, a fact that makes the efforts of the play's law officers to break up the gathering both gratuitous and shortsighted. A 49 is centrally a time for coming together, and coming together indeed is the model and the message of this play.

The opening scene, set about a hundred years ago, introduces Night Walker, a holy man and tribal leader. He calls to his people with a message that is extended and elaborated throughout the play. He talks to all his people, the spirits of the dead and the spirits of the yet-to-be-born, his ancestors and the future generations upon whom the survival of the nation must depend. Night Walker is the central character of the play, the mediator who calls himself both the oldest member of his tribe and the youngest, the magical center of all the nation's history. He carries traditional artifacts of prayer—tobacco, sage, and cedar—but his prayer does not depend on their presence alone; they may disappear and yet the people continue. With his shamanistic powers of foresight, Night Walker can observe, although not participate in, the events at the 49. He is fearful of what the future holds for his people but hopeful that strength will be found when it is needed. He recognizes that change must and will occur. But whether the change is "a loss that will be like death to our people" or an entry into "a time of understanding when a man will not hurt a man by killing his way of living" will depend on the strength and purpose of those who follow. Other aspects of tradition and continuity are represented by Weaving Woman and Singing Man, artists knowledgeable in the gifts of wool and color, of the drum, bell, flute, and rattle. Singing Man teaches that the power of song—and, by implication, all the power of the people—lies in the process of creation, not in the product. When he asks a boy and girl to "sing the song you have for each other," the boy replies, "It is a good song, but it is not finished yet." Singing Man responds: "I know many songs which are not finished. They are still songs." He knows that "our music is everywhere . . . you can find it wherever you look," just as Weaving Woman knows that the truth of a design is in the mind before it is in the rug: "A design can live and grow for many years before it is placed on the loom."

The play culminates in two beautifully balanced scenes, the first as quiet and measured as a heartbeat, the second violent and turbulent. In the first, Night Walker sits under an ancient arbor that draws its strength from the hearts and souls of the tribe and relates a parable set in an indefinite time in the past, when Indians suffered from a failure of creative energy and belief in themselves. A group of children listening to an old woman tell stories seems to vanish from inside a lodge. In a vision a holy man sees that the children are still safe and happy inside. Although at first he is not believed, he sits under the arbor and prays. Gradually the children take shape in the tipi, then emerge, saying: "We could see all of you but you could not see us. We could not come out until you believed that we were inside." The children in the tipi are types of the future generation who will not be able to realize their full potential as Indian people until there is a binding faith throughout the tribe.

The second scene begins with an apparently pointless, divisive fight between two young men at the 49. The police surround the clearing—the stage, in fact, for no police are ever in sight of the audience—in an attempt to break up the gathering. Suddenly, without planning, the group silently knits together and defies the police. They weave a constantly, subtly moving defense in the form of a great bird, an elaborate and living barricade against the outside intrusion. The police are irrelevant to the issue except as a catalyst; they simply provide the necessary focus for the coming together. The barrier that the dancers build is a realization of their faith in themselves and in their values, and that process of building is in itself where the value lies. The creative act of joining is the essence; the blockade is a trivial result.

Both scenes manifest a cycle of ritual death and rebirth as each group is confined in its enclosure of lodge or 49 ground. For those at the 49, however, the birth is more difficult because there has been a break in the continuity—"like a death," in Night Walker's words—and the sense of real community must be re-created. This continuing cycle of birth, death, and rebirth is maintained by faith, even if the links with the past are severed. Indeed, as the parable demonstrates, mere historical continuity is not enough; belief in and preparation for the future is essential. When they enter the 49 ground, the youths are divided and dispersed, spiritually, emotionally, and physically. One young woman wrecks her car in her haste to reach the 49, although her motives for being there are clearly shallow. A young man tries to impress his friends with a song but fails because he does not know it. And over all hangs a pall of pointless activity that wastefully dissipates the spiritual energy necessary for life and growth. In the confrontation with the police, however, the spirit and energy of the youths are focused on their common goal. The barrier is built dynamically, without words of anger and vituperation, and a deep understanding of their strength and purpose comes into being. This shared understanding is only a beginning—Geiogamah has no romantic vision of an instant utopia—but it is real and good. As the play ends, the shaman Night Walker appears with a bull-roarer and rattle and, with the power and fury of a storm, calls the youths "a tribe—of singers—of dancers who move with the grace of the bird—of people with strong hearts." The lesson, although delivered differently, is the same as that in *Body Indian*. By building a living pattern of pride and self-respect, by believing in the strength of their way, the people have become a nation again, renewing and re-creating the sacred bonds essential for their continuance as a people.

Although he is a Kiowa, Hanay Geiogamah writes plays for all Indian people. He purposefully draws on many cultures for the music used in the plays—Ute, Caddo, Salish, Navajo, Taos, Apache, and others. While the figure of Night Walker is not inconsistent with a traditional Kiowa holy man, he more cogently represents any highly respected leader and, beyond that, the collective and enduring wisdom of all Native Americans. Although Geiogamah occasionally uses Kiowa in his dialogue, it does not signal a restriction of the characters to a Kiowa situation, a fact that was dramatically underscored by the ensemble's acting company, whose members were drawn from a wide range of Indian groups. Nevertheless, there is an authentic and distinctive Indian voice in these plays, both in the diction, which preserves telling elements of Indian speech in English, and in the form and content of his dialogue. Geiogamah's linguistic skill is considerable. He can reproduce the maundering byplay of a sullen alcoholic without becoming tedious, and he can create the simplicities of Night Walker's language without becoming mawkish. Geiogamah understands and uses the history and literary techniques and traditions of Native American peoples while avoiding lurching cavalcades of wooden figures. Above all, there is a dignity and integrity to these plays, a sense in which the works themselves, funny and fierce, stand as examples of the philosophical and political values they promote.

NEW
NATIVE
AMERICAN
DRAMA

BODY
INDIAN

A PLAY IN FIVE SCENES

Body Indian

Body Indian was first presented at La Mama Experimental Theater Club in New York City on October 25, 1972, with the following cast:

BOBBY LEE	Bruce Miller
HOWARD	Timothy Clashin
THOMPSON	Phil Wilmon
MARIE	Marie Antoinette Rogers
EULAHLAH	Debbie Finley Snyder
ALICE	Jane Lind
ETHEL	Grace Logan
BETTY	Bernadett Track Shorty
MARTHA	Debra Key
FINA	Geraldine Keems
JAMES	Keith Conway

Directed by John Vaccaro
Set designed by Phil Wilmon
Lighting and sound by Mike Trammel
Theme song composed by Ed Wapp, Jr.
Drum and Rattle, Adrian Pushetonequa and Nelvin Salcido
Male Soloist, Adrian Pushetonequa
Female Soloist, Zandra Apple

The People
of the Play

BOBBY LEE, a crippled alcoholic in his mid-thirties
HOWARD, aged sixty-five or seventy, Bobby's Indian "uncle"
THOMPSON, same age as Bobby, overweight and obviously a
  heavy drinker
EULAHLAH, in her late twenties, Thompson's wife
MARIE, Bobby's cousin, Howard's downstairs neighbor
ETHEL, Howard's girlfriend, a "visitor"
ALICE, one of Bobby's "aunts," a middle-aged heavy drinker
BETTY, same as Alice
MARTHA, in her late teens, a hip young Indian "chick"
FINA, same as Martha
JAMES, in his late teens, Howard's grandson, Martha and
  Fina's sidekick

Setting

Howard's one-room apartment. A large old-fashioned bed dominates downstage center. Its mattress and loose coverings are dingy. Upstage right is the entrance door. Immediately right of the entrance stand kitchen props: a small two-burner stove, a one-faucet sink, and a table with oilcloth covering; they all look greasy, messy.

Stage left of the bed is a small mattress on the floor, spread out in pallet fashion. Above the head of the mattress and to the right of the table is a doorway to a bathroom, smaller than the entrance door.

Many empty liquor bottles are lying around the floor. Some of the labels are visible—Arriba, Lucky Tiger, Stag, all cheap wine brands. There are so many of these that the performers must stumble over and around them to make their way through the action of the play.

The railroad tracks and other special effects are provided by means of slides. Additional film effects for exterior scenes may be used at various points suggested by the text; for example, the Mint Bar where Bobby was with his aunts before arriving at Howard's, or the maiming tragedy on the railroad tracks.

Author's Note

The first scene should immediately establish the mood and tone for the rest of the play. It is important that an "Indian frame of mind" be established in the performances from the very start of the play. This is not something that the actors will build but something that they will sustain throughout. The following suggestions may be helpful.

1. Lines must be delivered in a clipped fashion, a kind of talk characterized by a tendency to drop final *g* ("goin'"), to jam words together ("lotta"), to add a grammatically super-fluous final *s* ("mens"), to leave a hiatus between a final and an initial vowel ("a old one"), and (in women's speech particu-larly) to lengthen vowels inordinately ("l—ots"). In no way whatever is anything negative or degrading intended; this is simply the way the characters in this play speak English. The actors should be warned against overplaying this "Indian" speech. It should never become garbled and unclear.

Definitions of Indian words used in the play:

Hites: a close friend, usually male, like a brother but not related by blood; one who has shared many life experiences with you.

Ka-zog-gies: a euphemism for "ass" or one's bottom. In this usage it is plural.

Pah-be-mas: a way of addressing as friends women who are not related by blood.

Ko-ta-kes: a misspoken euphemism for "brothers," or for

"brothers who've chosen each other as brothers," or, in a special usage, "blood brothers" without being kin by birth.
Haw: translates as "yes," an affirmative reply.
Pah-bes: Friends, buddies, "partners," in a special usage one's "brothers."
Al-hong-ya: money.

2. Group effort will produce both the proper restraint and gusto for the requisite Indian style of drinking. The drinking should be a controlled part of the entire performance; that is, the actors should be cautioned not to exaggerate the drinking movements, which must be performed as naturally as possible. Great swaggering and swilling of the bottles are more indicative of amateur acting than anything else. It is important that the acting nowhere is conducive to the mistaken idea that this play is primarily a study of the problem of Indian alcoholism. At moments in the play when much drink is available, the performers may take large drinks; when the supply is dwindling, the drinks are smaller or are sipped carefully.

3. The singing and dancing should be informal and improvised extensions of the characters' thoughts and moods. Not every song will be completed; some tunes will be hummed; some songs are cut off abruptly.

4. It is not necessary to distinguish what tribes the various characters belong to, but that there is a difference in tribes, and that the characters are aware of that difference, should be made obvious.

5. A certain degree of rollicking is permissible, but care must be taken not to overdo makeup, the poor quality of the clothing, gesticulation, the "Indian" speech traits, and all physical actions, most especially those used in the rollings.

6. There should be a loud, rushing sound of a train starting off on a journey to signal to the audience that the play is beginning, and Bobby's entrance can be emphasized by the distant sound of the train.

Scene 1

Bobby enters from stage left and crosses the stage on crutches. He knocks on the door unevenly. Onstage are Howard, Thompson, Eulahlah, and Ethel. Howard and Ethel are lying on a mattress on the floor. Thompson and Eulahlah are sleeping on the bed. Thompson rises slowly and sluggishly to answer Bobby's knock. Lights up from dim to bright as the door opens.

THOMPSON

> (*opening door*) Well, I'lll beee! B—obbye Leee! Come in, hites, come in! Long time no see. (*He reaches for Bobby's hand. They shake. Bobby lumbers into the room.*)

BOBBY

> Hey, guy, go down and *halp* my aunts up the stairs, will you? And pay that cab. I can't make it back down those stairs now. They're really iced. (*He hands Thompson money.*) My aunts are kinda' buzzin', halp them up the stairs. Don't let them fall on their ka-zog-gies. (*He smiles broadly.*) Say, tell that driver I want my sacks.

Thompson nods in agreement, puts on a shirt and shoes, and exits. Eulahlah stirs when the door shuts. Bobby sits down in the empty chair, exhales.

EULAHLAH

> (*groggily*) Weeelll Bobbyee Leee. Heeey. (*She gets off bed*

and goes to hug and kiss him.) Saaay, guy, last time—
(*cough stops her speech*). . . . Hey where's Thompson?

BOBBY

He went down to pay my cab. He's coming right back
up. He's halping my aunts up them stairs.

EULAHLAH

(*puzzled*) Your aunts?

BOBBY

Yeah, you know 'em. Betty and Alice.

EULAHLAH

Oooh, yeah, yeah, I know all of dem. I drank with Alice
'bout three days ago uptown. Yeah, I know dem, Bobby.

*She continues to fondle Bobby and peers around at the others
in the room, attempting to focus her eyes and gain composure
as she does so.*

BOBBY

(*nodding toward Howard and Ethel on the floor*) Heeey,
what's wrong with old guy there? Is he passed?

EULAHLAH

(*giggling*) Oh, no, he's sleep. He and Ethel's been
drinkin' for few days now, but he's not passed out now,
just sleep. He's got cold. Doctor at clinic told him he
better stay in bed for few days. He's been drinkin' l—ots
since he made his lease. I guess he got sick from drinkin'
too much wine. Thompson was thinkin' 'bout takin' him
to hospital at Lawton.

BOBBY

(*laughing lightly at this report*) When did he make his
lease?

EULAHLAH

'Bout two weeks ago. Or maybe a week ago. Thompson
hasn't made his yet.

10

BOBBY

> I just made mine this mornin'. But my damn lease man didn't want to pay me what I wanted. I was too broke to hold out, so I just signed it.

Bobby fumbles for a cigarette and takes some time lighting it. He sounds exhausted when he exhales. He smokes the cigarette with deep draws.

BOBBY

> I was goin' back to city today, but the roads are too bad. I saw my aunts at Mint and they told me Howard was over here. Is Marie down there?

Bobby gestures with his lip toward the floor, but Eulahlah doesn't seem to hear him. Noise is heard from the hallway outside. After many bumping sounds, the door opens and Thompson, Betty, and Alice enter. The women are frowzy. They are in a happy mood, carrying on loudly.

EULAHLAH

> (*gesturing broadly at the women*) Hae—ye! My pa-be-mas. Heey!

They all laugh lightly and exchange Indian women greetings.

THOMPSON

> (*with pleased smile*) Here's your sacks, Bobby. Soun's like you got jugs in there.

BOBBY

> I do.

BETTY

> Welll, helll, then, open one up!

They crack open a bottle by hitting it on the bottom and then removing the screw top, and begin to take long drinks as the wine is passed around. Drum and rattles come up as the drink-

ing begins. Howard and Ethel are awakened by the merriment. Howard rises from the bed, sees Bobby sitting in the chair, shouts a greeting, then moves arthritically toward Bobby and embraces him. Ethel greets the other women with wan enthusiasm. The bottle continues to be passed around uninterruptedly. Ethel approaches Bobby. The light percussion continues to the end of the scene.

ETHEL

H—ell—oo Bobby. How are you, sonny? You look preeety good. Haven't seen you in a lo—ng time, boy.

BOBBY

(*more settled now*) You're E—thel, annet?

ETHEL

Yeah, yeah, Bobby, it's me, E—thel.

BOBBY

You're kin to me, annet?

ETHEL

Yeah, yeah, Bobby, we're related. On my mother's side, I think.

BOBBY

(*traces of drunken slur beginning to show in his voice*) Your dad was my dad's Indian brother. Ko-ta-kes, haw! (*He makes an appropriate gesture with his hand.*)

ETHEL

Yeah, that's right, Bobby. Brothers!

HOWARD

(*interjecting*) Yeah, yeah, ya'll are kin. Ethel is related to your mother, Bobby. Your mother was my dad's sister. Ethel's dad was kin to both of them.

BOBBY

Yeah. That's the way it is . . . yeah.

HOWARD

Ethel here has a-been visitin' for few days now. Too cold to go back west. She's waitin' to make her lease.

BOBBY

(*continuing to drink from the bottle*) Is Marie down there?

HOWARD

Yeah, I think so. I heard her yellin' at them kids this mornin'. She had one of them with her when she was up here last night.

ALICE

I saw her uptown yesterday mornin'. I think she's been behavin' it.

The women laugh at this.

BOBBY

I need to see her. Need to talk to her 'bout signin' up for program at Norman. She's got to sign with me.

HOWARD

(*concerned*) She'll be up here. She'll hear us through the roof. She always come up here when she hear us talkin' and makin' noise.

BOBBY

Has she been drinkin'?

HOWARD

You know how she is.

Betty rises and carries bottle to Bobby. The others focus on her doing this. Drum and rattles come up.

BETTY

(*merrily*) Here, Bobby, take a b—ig drink. We haven't seen you in lo—ng time. Drink with us, Bobby.

Bobby grins, is pleased with Betty's attention. The others laugh and encourage him. He takes the nearly full bottle, turns it up, and downs the entire contents with a slow, steady gurgle. He gasps when he is finished. Another bottle is opened and starts the rounds. Bobby sits almost stupefied. Howard

13

*fawns over him. Bobby's teeth grit and streams of saliva run
from the sides of his mouth. The others pretend they do not
notice. Bobby slumps over the chair and passes out. Slowly
they all surround him. There is a menacing air as they do this.
The lights dim to a haze.*

HOWARD

> (*gently, to avoid waking Bobby*) Bobby. Hey, Bobby.
> Sonny, are you wake? You want 'nother drink? Bobby.
> Situp, sonny. Ethel wants to visit with you. (*There is no
> sign of life in Bobby. Howard moves in closer.*) Bobby.
> Bobby.

*They lift his body from the chair with drunken eagerness and
carelessness and carry him to the bed. One of the women
adjusts his legs so that he lies stretched out on the bed.*

HOWARD

> Bobby. Does your leg feel okay? Does it hurt you, sonny?
> Do you want us to take it off for you? (*He moves close to
> Bobby's ear.*) Bobby. We goin' run out of jugs. We got to
> go get some more. Bobby. You got any money, sonny?
> We goin' run out. Bobby, heeey, Bobby, can you help us
> out?

*Howard touches Bobby's leg, moves back, and motions to
Ethel to join him.*

HOWARD

> (*now certain that Bobby is thoroughly passed out*) This
> boy always pass out pretty fast. When he got his leg cut
> off and start wearin' that other leg, he start drinkin' pret-
> ty heavy. (*pause*) He was passed out on those tracks
> when he got hurt. (*pause*) I know he got money on him.
> He always hide it in that leg.

Howard and Ethel begin to search Bobby's pockets. They find cigarettes, folded papers, change, and two or three one-dollar bills.

ETHEL
    This ain't all he has!
HOWARD
    Feel in back.

Ethel puts her hand in Bobby's back pocket with a stealthy movement.

ETHEL
    He don't have no billfold. Wait, here's some. . . .

She pulls a few bills out, looks quickly to determine their denomination, and then moves quickly to cover her find.

HOWARD
    (*nervous*) How much was it?
BETTY
    Is there any more wine?

Howard and Ethel scuffle over the money.

ETHEL
    Just little bit.
BETTY
    Where?
ETHEL
    (*gesturing with her lips*) Over there . . . in those sacks.

As Betty rises to get the wine, the distant sound of a rushing train and whistle blasts from offstage. The cast freezes. The drum and rattles grow intense. Expressions of fear slowly cross over cast's faces as they look directly toward the audience.

15

ETHEL
I can hear it. Sounds like it's 'bout twenty, thirty miles away.

ALICE
I can barely hear it.

BETTY
I hear it little bit.

ETHEL
Hear it?

EULAHLAH
I can hear it ... now.

THOMPSON
Sounds like hummin'.

ALICE
The sound makes a little buzzin' feelin' on my ear.

BETTY
(to Howard) You hear it, Grampa?

HOWARD
(hobbling to downstage center) I can hear it just a little bit. Just a li—ttle bit.

Percussion sounds and lights intensify, then out. When the train whistle is heard, color slide projections of railroad tracks can appear, taken at varied sharp angles and flashing in rapid sequence, onto the back wall.

Scene 2

The lights come up with the company, except for Howard, sitting or lying all about the room. Howard is standing in the middle of the room with a bottle of wine in his hand. He is in a jolly mood, singing and joking with the others. Bobby is sitting at the edge of the bed, his position for most of the rest of the play. Empty bottles clutter the floor. Howard's fun is being supported by the others. There is no indication that anything wicked has taken place, or that there is a world beyond the shabby walls.

HOWARD

    (with aged gusto) I sure like to dance. One of my boys almost won first at the fair one time. He sure was good. *(He moves around.)* I taught all my kids how to sing. He can sing *(pointing to Bobby.)* He sure can hit those high notes. *(no reaction from Bobby.)* He can't drum, but he can sing.

The women begin to shout encouragement to Howard for his dancing.

HOWARD

    I saw in Darko[1] paper they havin' a b—ig dance at Carnegie tomorrow night. I'd sure like to go. But evreee

[1]Anadarko, Oklahoma

17

time this guy always get us stopped by the county laws!
(*He points directly to Thompson.*)

ETHEL

Are you going to war dance for us, Howard?

HOWARD

Any time now. (*They all laugh. The merriment increases.*) Just watch me!

Betty and Alice shake imaginary rattles. Ethel stands and makes supportive accompanying movement. Thompson pretends to drum.

HOWARD

Fancy dance! Eee-hah! Eee-hah! Eee-hah! Eee-hah!

BETTY AND ALICE

Yo-a-hio-ya, yo-a-hio-ya. (*Music rises offstage. The scene intensifies as Howard trips around the room with his dance.*)

HOWARD

(*loudly, breathlessly*) The drummers are gettin' ahead of me! Slow 'em down! (*There is no indication from Thompson that he hears this.*) Eee-hah! Eee-hah! Eee-hah!

BETTY AND ALICE

Yo-a-hio-ya, Yo-a-hio-ya.

Then, on cue, the dancing and singing stop abruptly with a rattle fadeout. The participants let out a whoop. While they have been carrying on, Marie has entered. The company all focus on her, and there seems to be an attitude of resentment toward her.

HOWARD

(*as if surprised, speaking directly to Marie*) Marieeeee! Come in! Come in! Come over here and sit down. Look who's here. Bobby's here.

Howard leads her to Bobby on the bed.

MARIE

(*suddenly*) Welll, hiii, B—obbyee. (*She kisses him.*)
Where have you beeen? I haven't seen you in so lo—ng.
I was startin' to get worried about you.

*The others arrange themselves, find bottles, eye Marie, but
one by one fall asleep. Meanwhile Bobby has been coming
around, and now sits up on the bed.*

BOBBY

(*adjusting*) I came down to make my lease. I can't go back
to the city today. Roads too bad. Thought I'd come here
to see if you was here. They tol' me you was here.

MARIE

I thought you was up here when I heard you walkin' on
the floor. I thought you'd be here for lease signin'. Did
you sign yet?

BOBBY

My damn white lease man wouldn't give me what I
wanted. I was gonna hold out, but I needed the money. I
had to sign for what he wanted to give me. I couldn't
help it.

MARIE

I'm gonna' make mine Monday. He already made his.
(*She lip-gestures toward Howard.*) You got any money
on you, Bobby?

BOBBY

I can spare you a little bit. I need all I have.

MARIE

I don't have any groceries. I tried to borrow some from
Howard the other day, but he didn't even have any ra-
tions left. Thompson and his wife stay here nearly all the
time now. He just barely gets by on that lease money of

19

his. Jobs are hard to find. 'Specially for Indians 'round here. You know how it is. Money's sure scarce.

BOBBY

I was gonna' tell you . . . (*pausing to drink*) . . . I want to use my lease money to get in program at Norman. It's a A-A deal for alcoholics. That preacher in the city told me they could dry me out in 'bout six weeks. I wanna' go over there. I need a relative to sign my papers with me. Can you sign them for me?

MARIE

Does your caseworker at the Bureau know about this?

BOBBY

(*angrily*) He doesn't have to know about it! I can go if I want to.

MARIE

Did they say you could go?

BOBBY

(*irritated*) I don't have to ask them. I can go on my own, but I have to have a relative to co-sign for me to get in.

MARIE

How much does it cost?

BOBBY

You can pay if you want to. I want to pay. It costs $400. I'll be in there for six weeks.

When Bobby mentions $400, some of the others stir and take notice.

MARIE

Do you have the papers with you, Bobby?

BOBBY

(*slurring his words*) I left them in the city.

MARIE

Do you want to lay down, Bobby?

BOBBY
> (*slumping, jerking, drooling*) Uuuhaa.

Bobby is again stupefied from the wine. Marie rises and lays him out on the bed. This takes some effort from her. She talks to him, though she knows he is passed out. Her speech begins to sound chilling. When she has him stretched out, her actions and speech quicken.

MARIE
> Bobby. Bobby! Bobby, are you sleep? Are you sleep, sonny? Bobby. Bobby.

While she is talking to Bobby, Thompson begins to move, as though drugged, toward the bed.

HOWARD
> He's sleep. I know he got money. Look in leg.

Marie and Thompson begin to search Bobby's pockets. They go over his entire body, leaving his clothes disheveled, and in the process pull up the pants over Bobby's artificial leg. Frantically they begin to compete to find money stashed in the apparatus. Thompson finds money, and Marie tries to grab it from him.

MARIE
> I need some of that!

THOMPSON
> No, uuuh, hey!

THOMPSON
> (*with a nervous, alcoholic twitch*) I'll check. I'll check . . . for . . . for all of . . . us. (*The others freeze.*) It . . . it's st . . . sti-ll there. Movin' this way. Comin' closer.

The visuals of the tracks appear again, then go out with the lights.

Scene 3

The lights come up with the women standing center stage in a round dance formation. They begin singing and dancing to the 49 tune of "Strawberries When I'm Hungry." Marie sits uneasily in the background, obviously not welcome to take part in the women's frolicking. As the scene progresses, the women's mood gradually becomes sadder, angrier, more desperate.

ALICE

I was gonna' camp at the fair this year, but Junior got throwed in 'bout a week before the fair started, and we couldn't put up our arbor. I sure like to hear that music comin' from the dance grounds.

BETTY

I haven't camped at the fair since I was a little girl. The dust bothers me, but I like the dancin'.

ETHEL

It's cheaper to camp than it is to live in town.

EULAHLAH

Daddy and 'em used to butcher before we came to the campgrounds. I really liked to fix up that meat.

ALICE

(*slowly*) I wish I had some meat now. My kids been eatin' only commodity meat for 'bout two months now. Junior's unemployment ran out a month ago. There ain't no jobs nowhere.

BETTY

Just be glad you have your gas and lights workin'.

ALICE

They will be for just couple of days more. I got my final notice that they was gonna' cut them off last week. That city truck will be pullin' up in the alley first thin' Monday mornin'.

ETHEL

(*reflecting*) I put my nephews in government school this fall. I sure didn't want to, but at least they get taken care of there. I hate for my kids to have to go without.

EULAHLAH

I didn't mind goin' to G I school so bad. Aayyee. (*The others smile knowingly at this.*) They treated me pretty good where I went. Some of those schools ain't so bad, but some of them sure no good.

ETHEL

My oldest nephew plays football at Riverside. His picture was in paper two or three weeks ago. I sure felt proud when I saw it in there.

ALICE

(*almost crying*) Everything is sure rough. I can't even get on state welfare. They say my husband is able to work. He's able, but there's no work.

BETTY

(*slowly*) All those white people think Indians have it good because they think the government takes care of us. They don't even know. It's rougher than they know. I'd like to trade my house for a white lady's house on Mission Street. I'd like for a white lady to have my roaches. You see them at the store, and they look at you like your purse is full of government checks. I wish my purse could be full of government checks.

ALICE
> I wish I had a check from anywhere.
> (*The bottle is moving around.*)

EULAHLAH
> So do I.

ETHEL
> So do I. I'd get my son out of county jail if I did.

The drumbeat comes up. Bobby has been watching the women as they lament. A pause while the bottle comes round to him, then he speaks.

BOBBY
> (*surprisingly alert*) Every Indian needs to have a government check for $25 thousand. They could give you womens $50 thousand. Then you could buy all your kids shoes, clothes, bicycles, pay rent, pay fines, buy shawls and earrings, and put the money you have left in the bank to live on. That's the only way you'd ever have the money you need.

The women turn their attention to Bobby as he makes this statement. They all laugh heartily as he finishes talking, then rise and surround him to tease him.

ETHEL
> Hey, Bobby, sonny. I bet you haven't 49'd in a long time. Come on, dance with us. You can dance with your crutches.

The women straggle into a round dance formation, pulling Bobby up onto the floor with them. He first resists, then gives in. Bottles are in hand. They begin to sing, in high-pitched voices, the 49 song "One-Eyed Ford," with Bobby singing along. As the dancing progresses, Bobby guzzles from a bottle and begins to falter, throwing the dancers out of kelter. One of his crutches flies across the floor as the women, with much fuss and giggling, lay him out on the bed. They stop singing and begin to glance at one another.

ALICE
> *(in low voice)* Sssssh. Sssssh. Hey, Bobby has some money, annet?

BETTY
> I think so.

ETHEL
> He does.

ALICE
> How much?

BETTY
> I think he's got lots.

ETHEL
> He signed his lease today.

EULAHLAH
> *(nervously)* He said he signed it.

ALICE
> *(to Howard)* Howard, does my nephew have any money?

Howard is nearly out and does not reply.

BETTY
> I know he'd help us out if he could.

ETHEL
> He's my relative. I know he'd help me out.

EULAHLAH
> Me and Thompson helped him out before.

ALICE
> He always comes to my house when he's here. I always take care of him.

ETHEL
> He used to stay with me long time ago. He was tryin' to get straightened up.

BETTY
He sure is a g—ood guy. Poor thing.

ALICE
You all must be good to him now, he's a poor thing. Y'all
be good to him.

BETTY
We'll be good to him.

ETHEL
Yeah, we will.

EULAHLAH
Oh, okay. We'll be good to him.

*The lights lower as they begin to search Bobby. They find a
few dollars, stuffing them into their bras as they do. When
Eulahlah fumbles with Bobby's artificial leg, Marie startles all
of them*

MARIE
I saw you!

*The women quickly return to their dancing and singing, pre-
tending they have not rolled Bobby. Their cackling cries
are drowned out by the offstage train whistle, this time
louder than before. The railroad tracks are projected over
them as they freeze in their dance pattern. The lights go out on
a slow count as the women clutch for each other, reach their
hands out toward the audience, then freeze again.*

Scene 4

A restlessness has settled over the group. They know that the wine supply is quickly dwindling. Eulahlah and Thompson quarrel; Ethel needles Howard.

BETTY

    I wish John was here. I haven't seen him . . . in 'bout a week now.

ALICE

    (*in same lonely tone*) Junior went lookin' for a job the other day. Somebody said they saw him at Erma's. He always shows up when he runs out of steam.

BETTY

    I hope John gets his business taken care of pretty quick. His lease man is a son of a bitch. He won't even give us an advance, even when we don't have groceries.

BOBBY

    (*coming suddenly to life and slowly, in drunken movements, searching himself*) Somebody took my money. It's almost all gone. (*pause*) I got to use that money to go to Central State at . . . Norman. (*pause*) What happened to it? . . . Who took it? (*shouting*) Howard? (*pause*) Where's . . . Marie? (*Marie makes a movement in his direction, but stops short.*) Where's wine? (*pause*) Who . . . took my . . . money? (*The group doesn't respond to any of his questions and seems not to hear them.*) Why did you do . . . it . . . take my al. . . . ? (*He*

begins to grit his teeth and his body tenses.) I want
... to ... go ... to Norman. My money ... money ...
is ... for Norman. Where is it? Which one of you?

*He slumps over on the bed, but doesn't pass out. He moans
and grunts for the next several moments. The group sits now
as though there were nothing else to do but wait for something
to happen. There is a knock at the door. Howard answers it.
The others watch. Enter James, Martha and Fina. The young
people are greeted with blank expressions. The youths shake
the cold off themselves, exclaim about the harshness of the
weather outside, and survey, with expressions of amusement
and awe, the scene in the apartment.*

JAMES
(*to Howard*) How are you, Grampa?
HOWARD
Pretty good, preeety good. What are y'all doing, sonny?
JAMES
I came up to see you, to ask you for some al-hong-ya.

*While they are talking, Martha and Fina approach Bobby on
the bed. James guides Howard, now besotted, to the floor
pallet.*

MARTHA
(*jostling Bobby*) Heeeey, Bobby Lee, wake up, guy.
Hey, it's me, Marty, your buddy. Wake up. Where you
been, dude? I ain't seen you in a long time.

Bobby raises his head, slowly recognizing Martha.

BOBBY
(*groggily*) Heeeeeey, what are you ... ? (*focusing on
Fina*) Who's this?

28

MARTHA
    Her name's Fina.

Fina and Martha giggle. They seem to have a special interest in Bobby.

BOBBY
    Is she kin to you?

MARTHA
    Yeah, she's my cousin.

Bobby takes a drink, offers one to Martha and Fina. He is pleased by the attention he is receiving from the two girls. Fina puts her arm enticingly around Bobby. He responds enthusiastically by dropping the bottle to the floor.

FINA
    (*low whisper to Martha*) He's kind of good-looking.

James is talking and laughing with Howard and Thompson, paying no direct attention to the activity on the bed. Howard occasionally glances sharply at it.

MARTHA
    (*giggly, bouncy, high*) You want some more wine, Bobby Lee? Where is it?

BOBBY
    Over there. (*He points to a sack on the floor. Martha moves to get it.*)

MARTHA
    (*to group, sitting blankly around the room*) Golll, y'all look like y'all've been partying for 'bout three weeks. I bet y'all've drunk a l—ot. (*big giggle*)

There is no response to her remark. Martha, James, and Fina now converge on the bed, happy that they have gotten this far.

FINA

(*to James*) Does your Grampa have any money?

JAMES

He didn't say.

MARTHA

Ask him again.

JAMES

Wait!

MARTHA

(*gesturing toward Bobby*) I bet he's got some.

JAMES

If he did it's probably all gone by now.

FINA

Check him out.

JAMES

You check him out.

MARTHA

Heeey! I sure wish I had twenty. We could get a case and some gas. And we could go to that concert in the city tonight. Get hiii! Aye!

The young trio all laugh at Martha's fantasy

FINA

If I had twenty dollars, I'd buy me a... a... a living bra! Aaaeee.

JAMES

Man, I just wish I had a twenty. And a lid. I wouldn't go to school for days. Aaaeee.

FINA

(*as she fondles Bobby's torso*) He's kinda good-lookin'. Aaaeee.

They giggle and tease each other as they get Bobby's body into place to roll it. The adults are paying no attention to any of this.

JAMES

> (*sternly*) Check his pockets!

MARTHA

> (*toward group*) They probably took all of it already.

JAMES

> (*to Howard*) Where's his money, Grampa? Grampa, hey, does he have any money? We need some bad, man.

HOWARD

> (*after a pause, without looking up*) Look in shoe.

They begin to fidget with the orthopedic shoe attached to the artificial leg, and Martha yanks out a bill.

MARTHA

> (*exclaiming at the size of the bill*) W—ow! We can really make it with this.

FINA

> How much is it?

No reply from Martha. She giggles to herself, then signals to James and Fina that they should leave. They put on their coats and prepare to hurry out.

HOWARD

> (*to James*) Sonny, where y'all goin'?

JAMES

> We're gonna' drive around for a while, see who's uptown. . . . There's a rock band playin' tonight.

Martha and Fina make giggly small talk with the rest of the company as they prepare to exit. The low bleat of the train whistle sounds offstage. The youths first react as if it is a part of their high but become gradually more concerned, agitated. The track projections flash on.

FINA

> (*giggly and ooeey*) W—ow. It's really hummin', makin' a kinda' buzzin' noise.

31

MARTHA

Ooooooh. It feels warm. I can feel it on my ear. Hey, this is weird.

The others onstage watch this silently, no movement.

HOWARD

Sonny, can y'all come back pretty soon? I want you to help me out. Will you come check on us?

JAMES

Yeah, uh, okay, Grampa. 'Bout couple of hours.

MARTHA

(*trying to feel the track projections with her fingers*) Psssst! Psssst! I bet these guys have been puttin' their hands on these to get a buzz. Aaaeee.

Giggles from James and Martha; others are frozen in place.

JAMES

We'll see y'all pretty soon.

MARTHA

Take it easy.

FINA

Y'all be good. Be careful.

Lights out, sound off when the door closes behind them.

Scene 5

The party is nearing its end. Bobby Lee has been rolled four times so far, knows that this has happened, but has remained helpless. It is apparent on the players' faces that they have forgotten everything that has happened in the previous four scenes, that they are unaware of their abuse of Bobby. They want only to keep the party going. A soft drumbeat is heard offstage throughout the scene.

HOWARD

(*bitterly*) I guess all the wine is gone. Is there any more anywhere?

ALICE

Is all the wine gone? I want another one.

EULAHLAH

It's not all gone, is it?

THOMPSON

You drank 'bout four bottles of it yourself.

HOWARD

(*to Thompson*) Look over there, under that chair. (*Thompson looks, finds nothing.*)

THOMPSON

I thought I saw somebody hide one under here.

HOWARD

You did. You hid it under here.

EULAHLAH

He hid it. He can drink more than all of us together.

HOWARD

I didn't hide any wine.

EULAHLAH

I know I didn't.

BETTY

Is there a bottle hidden 'round here? Is there one hidden? I thought there was more wine than this.

HOWARD

There was a lot of wine. There was 'bout ten, 'leven, maybe twelve bottles. We had a couple of bottles when Bobby came.

EULAHLAH

We had more than a couple of bottles, Grampa. Goll, there was a lot more than a couple.

ALICE

(*checking under the furniture*) There's another bottle somewhere. It's too cold to go back uptown to get more. There's another bottle somewhere. (*pause*) There's another bottle somewhere.

During this discussion about the wine, Bobby silently watches from the bed, following the movements of the others as they look for bottles.

BETTY

(*angrily*) We bought a lot of bottles when we stopped at the liquor store on the way here in the taxi. I know we bought a lot of them. Two sacks full!

HOWARD

(*to Marie*) Hey, hey you. Do you have anything to drink downstairs?

MARIE

I don't have any wine. You drank all of it when you were down there the other day.

Their searching becomes frantic.

EULAHLAH
If there's no more wine in this place, then somebody go
get some uptown.

*There is no response from the men. Now there is a silence.
Bobby continues to observe their movement.*

HOWARD
(*after all have become exasperated from searching*)
There's no more wine here. We drank it all up. If any of
you want some more to drink, one of us will have to go to
town to get it.

BETTY
One of you men go.

ALICE
Yeah, Thompson, you or Howard go get us some more
drinks!

EULAHLAH
(*sharply*) Goddamn you, Thompson, go get us some
more drinks! (*Thompson tries to push her away, but she
persists.*) Get us some more drinks, you damn lazy thing.
Go on! Get us some more.

HOWARD
(*to Thompson*) Yeah, sonny, you go get us some more to
drink. We don't have no more. Go 'head, go get us some
more. We can stay here and drink it. Go 'head.

The others encourage Thompson to go. Thompson gives in.

BOBBY
(*suddenly, startling them all*) Is there any more . . .
wine? I want another drink . . . I need another drink!

35

HOWARD

We goin' send after some more, Bobby. Thompson here is goin' after some more uptown.

Marie rises, goes to Bobby on the bed.

MARIE

Bobby, do you want to go downstairs to my house with me? Howard will help you down the stairs so you won't fall.

BOBBY

I want a drink!

MARIE

Come with me, Bobby. There isn't any more drinks here.

BOBBY

(*coming alive*) Yes, there is, there's another drink here. (*The others turn to Bobby when he says this.*)

HOWARD

(*loudly*) Sonny, did you say there's another drink here? Did you say there's a bottle here?

Bobby doesn't reply, reels in his wooziness.

MARIE

Come downstairs with me, Bobby. They drank up all the wine they had here. There isn't any more wine. Come with me, Bobby.

HOWARD

(*pushing Marie out of his way*) Did you say there's some wine left here, Bobby? Tell me where's it at.

ALICE

Come on, Bobby Lee, be a good chief, tell us where there's another drink. We done drank up all that we had. There's no more, sonny.

EULAHLAH

Bobby Lee, hites, come on, guy, share your drink with us. Geee. We always help you out when you need it. Help us out. Share with us.

Bobby tries to protect himself from their pummeling.

MARIE

Bobby, I'm going downstairs now. I got to check on those kids. Howard will help you down the stairs. Come on down with him. I'll fix you a place to sleep. (*She waits for a reply; there is none.*) Howard, you must bring him downstairs. He doesn't need to drink any more. He can sleep for a while. Bobby, you come down with Howard. He'll help you down the stairs. These people are just gonna' keep on drinkin'. Come on downstairs.

Bobby remains silent. The others say nothing to Marie as she exits. They wait for Bobby to say where the wine is hidden.

HOWARD

Bobby, do you want to go down to Marie's?

BOBBY

No! No! I'm . . . okay, here.

HOWARD

Bobby, sonny, where's that wine at?

Bobby smiles faintly at Howard, then reaches slowly into his jacket and pulls out a full pint of wine, holds it up for all to see.

BOBBY

Here's wine. Y'all know I always have something hidden on me . . . to drink. (*They all laugh, pretending to accept this as a joke.*) If you drink, you should . . . you should always keep a small one hid on you. If you can.

He opens the bottle and drinks it all in one long gulp. The others push and claw for the bottle, but Bobby, fending them off with his free arm, keeps it out of their reach.

THOMPSON

> (*almost crying*) Hey, hey, Bobby Lee, hites, save me . . . save (*as last drop drains from bottle*) COR-NERRRS![2]

Bobby laughs drunkenly.

EULAHLAH

> (*with pain*) Ooooooooh, no!

The grip of needing a drink now tightens on all of them. Some of them show signs of "shakes."

HOWARD

> Thompson, go get us another drink.

THOMPSON

> (*trembling, sweating*) Okay, Okay! Give me money and I'll go.

HOWARD

> You have money to buy it.

THOMPSON

> I don't have any money. I'm broke.

EULAHLAH

> Me and Thompson don't have any more money. We spent it all a long time ago. You have money.

HOWARD

> I spent all my lease money already.

EULAHLAH

> No you didn't! You still have money!

---

[2]The last little shot, the final drops that usually collect in the corner of the bottle.

Courtesy of Ellen Stewart

ETHEL

> (*joining Howard, to Eulahlah*) We don't have any
> money. Howard's broke. (*pointing to Betty and Alice*)
> They have money!

ALICE

> I don't have any money. I've been broke for the past two
> weeks. I wish I had some money.

BETTY

> (*sadly, to Bobby*) I don't have... any... money.

THOMPSON

> No money, no drinks!

HOWARD

> Which one of you has a couple of dollars? (*No reply from
> any of them.*) I know somebody's got some.

THOMPSON

> Who's gonna' give me the money?

*Now everybody searches their pockets or purses to look for
money. They find nothing. Bobby moans. A loud knock on the
door. Howard answers. The three youths enter. They are now
more spaced out than previously.*

JAMES

> (*smiling, glassy-eyed*) You said to come back, to check on
> you all, didn't you, Grampa?

*The two girls eye Bobby on the bed, apparently to check his
vulnerability once again.*

HOWARD

> Yeah, yeah, I wanted you kids to come back to check on
> us. Sonny, do you have any al-hong-ya on you?

JAMES

> (*surprised*) Al-hong-ya? No, I don't. Remember, I asked
> you for some when we came here before.

HOWARD
> Yeah, yeah, but do you have any money? We need another drink.

JAMES
> We're all busted.

He giggles. The girls are waiting, talking with the others.

HOWARD
> Are y'all in your car, sonny?

JAMES
> Yeah, uh, huh. We been slidin' around in it uptown.

HOWARD
> What time is it, sonny?

JAMES
> It's early, man.

HOWARD
> Are those stores still open?

JAMES
> Yeah, they're open, the ones you want. (*He giggles again.*)

HOWARD
> (*looking around*) We sure need some money.

JAMES
> What do you want us to do?

HOWARD
> Sit down, y'all, sit down.

Howard now takes control, his grimness exerting a force over the others.

> Y'all know how Bobby Lee gets when he's been drinkin' for a long time and runs out. (*They all indicate that they know what he's talking about.*)
> He gets real sick, haw?

(*more agreement*) I was with him one time in Oklahoma
City jail when he got sick, real sick. He was really havin'
those dee-tees. His arms was movin' and jerkin', like
cow's when you butcher it. His legs was a-shakin'. He
soun' like he was chokin'. (*He strains for composure,
coughs, trembles.*) He tol' me he saw in his dee-tees a
row of lillel' chickens sittin' on those jail bars singin'
Indian songs.
He said they was purple and gold and red colors.
He said he felt like his head was bein' hit with a big iron
'bout ever so often.

The two girls giggle at the bizarre images Howard is describing.

He said he felt like he was fallin' through the whole
jailhouse floor into the sewer lines.
He said his hair was long as an old lady's, and his fingers
were all shrunk up, like he was a-dead.
He tol' me he thought he was goin' die while he was in
those dee-tees!
I don't want him to have them again! He's had them lots
of times.
I know what they're like. He's going have them again if
he don't get a drink.
He don't have any more al-hong-ya. It's all gone. He
spent it all. He always spen' his money fast.
He don't have any more wine hid.
I'm goin' get him some more wine before he wakes up.
He's goin' need it. (*pause*) He sure is goin' need a drink
when he wakes up. Y'all know that!

*Howard moves to the bed. He signals Thompson to join him.
They begin jostling Bobby's body roughly, almost brutally.
The others begin, one by one, to rise and stand around the bed*

to watch, hiding the operation from the audience. There is complete silence. Out of the audience's view, Howard and Thompson are removing Bobby's artificial leg. James is the first to leave the encirclement, signaling his two companions that it's time for them to leave. Howard calls James back for him to assist in rearranging Bobby's body on the bed.

HOWARD

> (*to James*) Sonny, I want you to take us to white man bootleggers on Washington Street. He'll give us what we need for this (*indicating artificial leg*). He'll let Bobby have it back when Bobby can get it out.

JAMES

> (*disgust in his voice*) Okay, let's hurry. It's gettin' late. We gotta' go to the concert.

Howard and Thompson prepare to leave, placing the artificial leg upright against the bed. Complete silence until Howard and Thompson are posed at the door with the leg wrapped in a dingy blanket. Drum and rattles now begin a gradual rise to the end of the scene. The youths have exited.

HOWARD

> (*to those who remain behind*) Y'all wait here. We'll be back pretty soon.

They exit. The women begin to straighten the room, to sweep, to pick up bottles. The track visuals appear in sharp contrast over Bobby's stretched-out body. Some time passes while the women clean before the train whistle is heard. The sound grows louder and awakens Bobby. He feels around on his body and discovers that his artificial leg has been removed. He pulls himself up, speaks increasingly louder so as to be heard over the train sounds. The women do not hear him. There is a sardonic smile fixed on his face.

43

BOBBY

Welll, h—ell—o, Bobby Lee. How are you, hites?
Lo—ng time no . . . seee.

He reaches for his crutches, has trouble securing them. Sitting upright on the edge of the bed, he looks straight ahead at a flashing train light, an entirely different mood about him now as horror overtakes him.

BOBBY

I can hear . . . a . . . train . . . that . . . train . . . my leg . . .
that train's gonna' . . . gonna hit . . . . . . my . . . . . . ley—g!

He slumps over as loud blasts from the train echo through the theater. The women continue tidying the room. Train sounds subside, lights begin to dim. The track visuals fade out. Silence.

END

FOGHORN

Foghorn

Foghorn was first presented at Theater Im Reichskabarett, West Berlin, Germany on October 18, 1973, with the following cast:

Jane Lind
Bruce Miller
Marie Antoinette Rogers
Irene Toledo
Maggie Geiogamah
Phillip George
Charlie Hill
Denice Hernandez
Luis Romero
Carpio Bernal

Directed by John Vaccaro
Production Stage Manager, Kenn Hill
Sets by Joe Peroni and Larry Rutter
Costumes by Margo Lazzaro

The People of the Play

NARRATOR, a spokesman for the Indians
NUN
ALTAR BOY
SCHOOLTEACHER, circa 1900, in stars and stripes skirt
THE PRINCESS POCAHONTAS
POCAHONTAS'S HANDMAIDENS, three or four
LONE RANGER
TONTO
FIRST LADY OF THE UNITED STATES
U.S. GOVERNMENT SPY
VOICE OF THE SPY'S CONTACT, (can be acted)
BULL
GIRL (reading treaties)

Wild West Show

SHOW CARD GIRL
HEAD WARRIOR
TWO INDIAN BRAVES (performing "hand-to-hand" combat)
TWO CHIEFS AND ASSORTED BRAVES (for Indian war council)
INDIAN INTERPRETER
LOVELY WHITE MAIDEN (wearing bright blonde wig)
LECHEROUS INDIAN MAN (who chases her)

Music

ELECTRONIC COMPOSITION FOR JOURNEY (4 or 5 minutes)
ZUNI SUNRISE CHANT
PLAINS INDIAN WAR DANCE SONG
VERY LOFTY CHURCH-ORGAN MUSIC (Nun Scene)
GOOD MORNING TO YOU (Schoolteacher Scene)
THE STAR SPANGLED BANNER (Schoolteacher Scene)
THE INDIAN LOVE CALL (Pocahontas Scene)
WILLIAM TELL OVERTURE ("Lone Ranger" Theme)
AMERICA THE BEAUTIFUL (First Lady Scene)
PASS THAT PEACE PIPE (AND BURY THAT HATCHET) (Special
Arrangement)
WILD WEST SHOW ACCOMPANIMENT (special composition on
show organ or piano; mock drumming rhythms for Indian
Council of War, Authentic Indian War Dance, and Savage
Brutal Scalp Dance. Old-fashioned piano for chasing of
Lovely White Maiden.)
THE AIM SONG ("Indian people will be free When we win at
Wounded Knee")

Author's Note

Almost all the characters in this play are stereotypes pushed to the point of absurdity. The satire proceeds by playful mockery rather than bitter denunciation. A production should aim at a light, almost frivolous effect (the basic seriousness of the play will emerge all the more effectively if the heavy hand is avoided). The actors should never appear to be preaching, nor should they strive too much for laughs; they should simply let them occur.

It is vital that there be a minimum of delay between scenes. The drilling sounds and the visuals of earth being drilled form a bridge between scenes, but they should be kept brief.

The stage can be decorated to reflect a mixture of the prison yard on Alcatraz Island during the 1969–71 occupation; the terrain around Wounded Knee, South Dakota, during the 1973 incident; a composite Indian reservation; and various national monuments across the United States, such as Mount Rushmore and the Jefferson Memorial. The visuals are intended to counterpoint the action and to give a feeling that the audience is actually present yet not directly participating in the action of the play.

It is desirable that the actors know how to sing, for live performance of the songs makes for a much stronger production. Some of the songs, such as "Pass That Peace Pipe and Bury That Hatchet," can be recorded on tape and the performance synchronized with them. The Wild West Show composition should almost certainly be taped. All traditional drumming should be performed live if possible.

It is not important if the audience can see offstage into the wings or if other elements of the production are exposed. The actors should pay no attention to this informality and take any accidents that may occur in their stride.

There should be a lot of color, but not so riotous that it distracts the attention of the audience. Props should be of slapstick proportions in the Nun, Peace Pipe, and Wild West Show scenes.

1

The opening section of the play, until the appearance of the religious personnel, is performed against a background of progressive electronic sound, one that evokes a journey through time and space, perhaps composed on a synthesizer or possibly with string instruments and percussion. The performing group follows a stylized choreography that is patterned to follow the electronic score. The "parts" are distributed among members of the performing group who form an ensemble for the production. They carry bundles of belongings, pull travois, and so forth. The costumes and movement should suggest a forced journey, such as the Trail of Tears, spanning the centuries from 1492 to the present and stretching geographically from the West Indies to Alcatraz Island. The delivery of the first six statements must be timed as a narration for the journey, and must convey an evolving attitude toward Indians. If enough performers are available, the company members can portray the Spanish sailor, senator, and others in spotlighted areas about the stage. Or the lines can be recorded on tape with the electronic score.

The stage is dark. Suddenly a large, painted Indian face appears, apparitionlike, moving slowly as it is projected about the stage, its eyes gazing toward the audience. The electronic music begins.

SPANISH SAILOR
>(*very excited*) ¡Señor Capitan Columbus! ¡Mire! ¡Mire!
>¡Mire! ¡Alla! ¡Mire! ¡Dios mio! ¡Estos hombres, cho-co-
>la-tes! ¡Los indios! ¡Los indios! ¡Ellos son los indios!

*The face fades as lights come up dimly, revealing the perform-
ing group frozen in position onstage. They begin moving
slowly as the electronic journey music resumes.*

MALE SETTLER
>You're only an Injun. Don't talk back! (*now louder*)
>You're only an Injun! Don't talk back!

*Sounds of mixed gunfire: rifles, old muskets, and so forth,
followed by a pause. Then more gunfire.*

TWO WHITE MEN
>(*voices colliding*) Vermin! Varmits! Vermin! Varmits!
>Vermin! Varmits!

Electronic journey music, group movement.

FEMALE SETTLER
>Filthy savages. Murderers! Scalpers!

Electronic journey music, group movement.

ANGRY MALE VIGILANTE
>I say let's force 'em off the land! Move 'em with force,
>guns! Now!

*Electronic journey music, group movement, mixed gunshots,
high volume. Electronic journey music and group movement
continue. More gunshots. Electronic journey music and group
movement now becoming fragmented.*

UNITED STATES SENATOR
>The Indian problem is a matter for the courts and the
>Congress to deal with. We've been victorious over them

Photograph by Chris Spotted Eagle

on the battlefield, now they must settle on the reservations we have generously set aside for them. They have stood in the way of our great American Manifest Destiny long enough.

Electronic journey music concludes as performers exit.

2

The performing group returns to the stage one by one as a panoramic view of Alcatraz Island is projected onto the cyclorama or back wall of the playing area. Photographs of the occupation are seen in a dissolving sequence as the group sings the Zuni Sunrise Chant.

GROUP

Following a leader, with respectful expressions
BAH HEY BA HO
BAH HEY BA HO

EYE YA NE NAH WAY
EE I YA HO. I YA HO WAY.
SHEY-NE NAH-WAY.

BAH HO. BA HEY.
BA HO. BA HEY.

NARRATOR

Thanksgiving Day, 1969. Alcatraz Island, San Francisco Bay. We are discovered, again. It was the first time that we had taken back land that already was ours. Indian people everywhere felt good about our having the island, about our determination.

The visuals continue, their projection punctured by the silhouettes of the performing group members, who stand attentively about the playing area.

We planned to develop the island, to build a cultural and spiritual center for all tribes, all people. Nineteen months. It was a good beginning.

Alcatraz fades. A gigantic map of the United States, blank except for delineations of the Indian reservations, comes into focus. The performing group now pantomimes boarding a boat, sailing across the bay. A low flute is heard. The players form a phalanx across the front of the stage as they disembark, and the narrator moves to downstage center.

Photograph by Chris Spotted Eagle

NARRATOR

We, the Native Americans, reclaim this land, known as America, in the name of all American Indians, by right of discovery. We wish to be fair and honorable with the Caucasian inhabitants of this land, who as a majority wrongfully claim it as theirs, and hereby pledge that we shall give to the majority inhabitants of this country a portion of the land for their own, to be held in trust by the American Indian people—for as long as the sun shall

55

rise and the rivers go down to the sea! We will further guide the majority inhabitants in the proper way of living. We will offer them our religion, our education, our way of life—in order to help them achieve our level of civilization and thus raise them and all their white brothers from their savage and unhappy state.

3

The performing group loudly sings and drums a Plains Indian War Dance song in celebration. When the singing ends, an organ blasts out church music, bringing on a Catholic nun and Indian altar boy, who carries a cross covered with paper money. Members of the performing group, wrapped in blankets and with poker-faced expressions, take places right and left of the nun and altar boy who are standing stage center, smiling.

NUN

(As church music fades, she speaks first calmly, then gradually up to a frenzy.)
My blessed savages.
Children of the unknown, of the wilderness.
You are most fortunate that we have found you.
You have been smiled favorably upon by the holy father in Rome.
He has seen fit to send us out to this New World to impart the divine wisdom of God to you. *(She pauses, fondles her book, then raises it in front of the Indians.)*
This book contains all of His holy teachings.
I am going to give His teachings to you.
For no soul must be without knowledge of the Almighty.

Photograph by Chris Spotted Eagle

No soul must be allowed to wander in the darkness, as
yours have for so long, and never know the Kingdom of
God.
You do not have religion!
You do not have an all-forgiving father like ours.
You are heathens.
Pagans.
Poor, miserable, ignorant, uncivilized, NAKED!
(*she calms herself.*)

We are going to take you out of this darkness and show you His way. And you will be happy and grateful, forever, that we have found you.

Our faith, our beautiful faith, that has been the salvation of so many millions of souls, will now be yours.

For without faith in God, the one, true Christian God, you will never have the hope of becoming civilized, of knowing a way of life other than this pitiful existence of yours.

And!

If we did not find you, your souls would burn! Burn forever, for eternity! In HELL!

She and the altar boy, who has been raising and lowering the cross behind her as she is speaking, now stand triumphantly before the group. The Indians attack them as the church music blasts through the theater. Then a sharp drilling noise is heard, the lights flash, and action visuals of giant chunks of earth flying through space are projected on the playing area.

4

A clownish schoolteacher dances onstage, ringing a bell, carrying a bundle of small American flags, singing "Good Morning to You." She has been preceded by a group of very young Indian students who run onstage playfully, taking seats on two wooden benches. They respond to the teacher with awe, surprise, mild defiance, and fear. The teacher is snobbish, nervous, rude, feisty, and blusterous.

TEACHER

(*very overdone, but with control*) Good morning, boys and girls, er, squaws and bucks. Good morning.

(*She puts the bell down, fusses with her hair and dress. The students pay no attention. She becomes angry.*) G—ood morning, savages! (*She busily arranges them in "order."*) I see that this is going to be more difficult than they told me it would be. You are all totally ignorant. You might as well be deaf and dumb! Do any of you understand any English? Not a single one of you?

(*to the audience*) I wonder if the people in Washington really know what they're doing by trying to teach these savages how to speak English, how to live like civilized human beings. These stupid children should be left on their reservations and forgotten about. What a bunch of worthless things.

(*She sees one of the girls gesture to one of the others, and pummels the girls, who pulls back wide-eyed with surprise.*) What are you doing there? What was that? Was that an Indian sign-language gesture I saw you making there? Was it? Was it sign language? Well, there won't be any more of that in this classroom, none of that! I'll rap your knuckles hard if you do that again. Do you hear me? Do you understand me? It'll be the dark room for you. (*pause*) That's one step out of savagery for you.

(*Suddenly pinching her nose in broad gesture*) Ooooooooh, oooooh! What an odor! (*She lifts the blanket of a girl pupil.*) Ooooohweeeeee, young lady, ooooohweeeee! You don't smell like a white woman! You smell like a... like ... a... Oh, my goodness, you are going to have to learn how to take a nice, civilized ladylike bath and keep your body clean. Do you hear me? That will be another step out of your darkness!

(*looking in one of the boys' hair*) Oh, heavens alive! Oh,

good heavens! Nits! Nits! Oh, and they're alive, they're real! Oh, oh! Lice! How disgusting, how utterly disgusting! (*She scratches herself wildly.*) Well, this can be easily solved. Everyone of you, everyone of you will have your hair cut off tonight. Tonight! Girls and boys. We will not have a bunch of lousy Indians in this classroom! No, oh, no!

(*after a short pause*) Sign language! Stinking bodies! Blankets! Deaf and dumb! How did these people ever get themselves in this condition?

The students are giggling again, she reestablishes order, continues.

You Indians are going to become educated, educated! That's spelled E-D-U-C-A-T-E-D, ed-u-ca-ted! Here in this school you are going to learn the English language. You are going to learn how to be Christians, how to worship God and live a clean, wholesome, decent life. You are going to learn how to be civilized people, civilized Indians, Indians who can earn an honest living, Indians that the American people can be proud of, not shamed by, so that we can hold our heads up high and say, "They are just like us, they are civilized. They aren't wild and on the warpath anymore. They are living the American way."

(*She sings a line of "Star Spangled Banner," then sees the girl make the gesture again, lunges at her, yanks up the child, shouts directly into her face.*) This is not the reservation, child! This is not that awful place you came from where you all run around half naked, filthy, living in sin! This is a white man's schoolhouse. I told you not to do that again. I told you what I'd do. (*She shakes the child violently.*) You are going to be a lesson for the others. You, child, are going to be punished. (*She pulls out a bottle of castor oil and pours it down the struggling child's mouth.*) It's the dark room for you. (*She pushes the child into a dark closet space.*) You will stay in here all day. No food! No water! And no toilet! (*turns to others*) She is a lesson for all of you to follow. I caught her doing a sign-language gesture. No more of that in his classroom, do you hear me? You are going to forget all of your Indian ways, all of them. You can start erasing them from your minds right now, right here, right this instant. No more of your disgusting sign language. No more of your savage tongue. No more greasy, lousy hair. No more blankets. You are going to learn the English language. That is what you were brought here for. (*turning to the audience*) The English language. The most beautiful language in all the world. The language that has brought hope and civilization to people everywhere. The one true language, OUR language!

(*Quickly turning her back to the students*) Now, listen to me carefully, very carefully. I am going to teach you your first word of English. Listen carefully, for it is the word, the one word, you must know first to become civilized. You must say this word to all of the white people you see, all of them, men and ladies. They'll be proud of you when they hear you say it, yes, proud, and when they hear you say it, they'll know that you are being relieved of your savage, uncivilized ways. They'll smile back at you and say the same thing. All right? Okay? Listen closely. The word is hell-o. Hell-o. H-E-L-L-O. Hello. Listen to the way I say it. Hello. Hell-o. It's the first word of the American way. The American way begins with hello. Say it, children, say it. Hell-O. Hell-O.

One of the pupils timidly tries the word and giggles as the others show amusement. The teacher hears her, yanks her to the front of the class with much flourish.

She said it! She said it! She said the word. She's on the road to the American way now! She said hello!

The teacher hands the girl a small American flag, then takes it back to demonstrate how to wave it while repeating hello. The girl clowns crudely with the flag in her hand as the teacher turns to coax the class one by one to say hello. The students ape the teacher with strong gestures as she continues to instruct the remaining students. The teacher soars on her success. The pupils form into a tight group, fists clenched, close in on her, and attack. The lights fade on the drilling sound, earth visuals.

5

The Princess Pocahontas runs onstage carrying flowers and singing "The Indian Love Call." Her handmaidens follow, giggling. As Pocahontas flutters about, the handmaidens seat themselves in a semicircle for gossip.

HANDMAIDENS
(*very eager*) How was it, Princess Pocahontas? How was it? Tell us.

POCAHONTAS
(*a languid smile on her face*) I couldn't take my eyes off him when I first saw him. He was so . . . so . . . ooh!

The handmaidens twitter excitedly, Pocahontas flutters back and forth.

HANDMAIDENS
So, so what, Pocahontas? Tell us, please.

POCAHONTAS
(*gesturing with her hands*) He was so . . . big. Ooooooh, uuuh.

HANDMAIDENS
(*puzzled*) Big? How do you mean, Pocahontas, big?

POCAHONTAS
(*enjoying the handmaidens' curiosity*) He had such big legs. Such big, uh, arms, such big, uh, uh, chest. Such big, big head. Such big, big hands. Such big, big feet. Such big eyes. Such big mouth. Such big ears. Ooooooh, aaahaaa.

HANDMAIDENS
And? And?

POCAHONTAS
And his hat was big. And his cape was big. And his boots and his sword and his. . . . And all of the other white men with him were big. Ooooooooh, uuuh.

The handmaidens squeal loudly as they pant for more details.

POCAHONTAS
(*eyes becoming dreamy*) Be quiet and I will tell you about the big captain. The big, big captain.

The handmaidens calm down, move in closer to hear.

POCAHONTAS
First, first he took me to his dwelling and he seemed, uh, kind of, of nervous about me being with him. He told one of the other captains that nobody was to . . . to come into the hut. This made me a little bit afraid at first, but he took hold of my hand and smiled at me. He kept smiling at me, and then he asked me, he asked me if I was a . . . a . . . vir-gin. When he said enough so that I

knew what he was talking about, I... I said to him,
"Yes, yes, I am a vir-gin." When I said this, he seemed
to get kind of nervous, excited. He looked at me deeply
with his big blue eyes and told me that he was... in
... in *luff* with me and he wanted me to... to... know
his body and that he wanted to know, know my body too.
Then he pulled me gently down on the bed and began to
put his lips on mine. He did this several times, and each
time his breathing became more, more nervous, like he
was getting very warm. Then he began to kiss my neck
and my cheeks. (*The handmaidens urge her on.*) And
then he touched my breasts. And then he stood up,
suddenly, and began to take off his clothes. He took off
his boots, his shirt, his pants, all that he was wearing. He
stood over me, his big, big, big body naked like one of
the little children. There was so much hair on his body,
it made me a little afraid. (*She giggles to herself.*)

HANDMAIDENS
(*interrupting*) Did you... did you take off... ?

POCAHONTAS
Yes, I did, slowly, I didn't know what... I was doing,
but I felt happy and warm and...

*One of the older handmaidens casts an unbelieving glance to
one of her companions on the last remark.*

HANDMAIDENS
Yes, yes! Tell us all of it!

POCAHONTAS
And the big captain was standing above me, looking
down at me, breathing like a boy after a footrace, and I
saw that his...

*The handmaidens huddle closely with Pocahontas for the in-
timate details. One of them pops up, exclaiming "Pink?" Then*

Pocahontas rises above them, lifts her arms in a manner to suggest an erect phallus. The handmaidens gasp. Then a kazoo whistle indicates that the erection falls quickly, and the handmaidens explode with laughter.

POCAHONTAS
(*fighting for their attention*) He said to me, I love you, dear Pocahontas. I promise you it won't happen the next time, I promise, I promise, I promise.

The lights fade on the handmaidens squealing with laughter. Drilling sound, earth visuals.

6

Tonto and the Lone Ranger enter with horse-riding pantomime as a piano thumps out familiar Lone Ranger theme. Piano stops and starts, giving Tonto an opportunity to make mocking gestures toward the Lone Ranger. Entrance music ends; they dismount. Lone Ranger takes a seat, exhales, motions to Tonto to shine his boots.

LONE RANGER
(*worried*) You know, Tonto, I've been thinking.

TONTO
(*impassively*) Kemo Sabay.

LONE RANGER
I've been thinking, Tonto. The way you always bail me out of the crisis right at the last minute with your clever thinking sure doesn't look too good for me. You know what I mean? It looks maybe like I'm not too smart having to rely on an illiterate Injun like you to do all the clever thinking, and even outsmarting the white man.

TONTO
> (*briskly shining the boots*) Kemo Sabay.

LONE RANGER
> Tonto, can you think of any way that I can come to your rescue and save you from the hands of death? Just once, Tonto? I'm really feeling insecure about this, old partner. You always come up with something good.

TONTO
> Kemo Sabay.

LONE RANGER
> People might start losing faith in me if they keep seeing you doing all the smart stuff. It's bad for business, Tonto.

TONTO
> (*shifting to Lone Ranger's other boot*) Kemo Sabay.

LONE RANGER
> (*inspired*) I got it! I got it! (*piano interlude suggesting wickedness, villainy*) Tonto, you get shot, real badly, right smack in the chest by a no-good Injun varmit who says you stole his squaw. You're about to die, and I find you. I get you to a friendly rancher's house, one where they'll let me bring my Injun friend inside, and do an operation on you to remove the bullet. How's that, Tonto?

TONTO
> Kemo Sabay.

LONE RANGER
> (*excited*) You're just about to bleed to death, and I know all this doctor's learning about surgery. Your life is fast slipping away. I'm trying hard to save you, me in my mask and my doctor's outfit and my scalpel and other tools, and suddenly you rise up to tell me which aorta in your heart to bypass, and the shock from this kills you instantly, and you fall back, dead. And, and, and I say: "I did what I could for my Injun friend, I tried to save him.

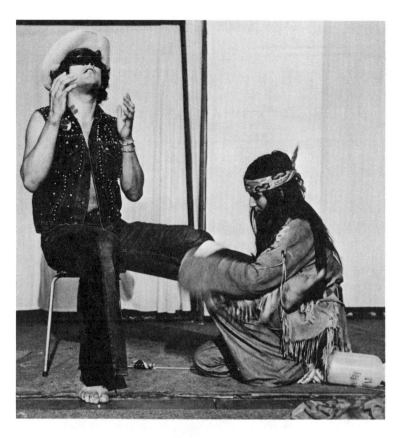

Photograph by Chris Spotted Eagle

I almost did, but he killed himself before I could finish the operation." How's that? Huh, Tonto, how's that? That'll show I'm not so reliant on you, right? It'd be the end of the Lone Ranger and Tonto, his faithful Injun companion. Then, there'd be just the Lone Ranger. How's that, Tonto? Sound like it'll work to you?

*The Lone Ranger stands staring out toward the audience,
caught up in the story. Tonto rises from the floor, taps him
lightly on the shoulder, he turns, and Tonto cuts his throat
with a knife. Drilling sound on tape, earth visuals, lights out
fast.*

7

*The performing group becomes an audience for a dedication
ceremony. "America the Beautiful" is heard, then scattered
applause, all on tape.*

DEEP MALE VOICE
> (*velvety and awestruck, on tape*) Ladies and gentlemen,
> I give you, the First Lay—dee of the United States.

Thunderous applause.

FIRST LADY
> (*A bit daffy and with fluttery happiness "to be here."*)
> Thank you. Thank yooou. I want to say right away that I
> have never seen such lovely, stoic faces as those of our
> Indian friends here with us today. Just look at those
> beautiful facial lines, those high cheekbones, those won-
> derfully well-rounded lips, those big dark eyes. And
> their costumes. Aren't they simply tooo beautiful?
> Let's-give-them-a-big-hand-ladies-and-gentlemen, let's
> give-them-a-big-hand. (*The Indians applaud, rib each
> other.*) Their radiance has made this day truly one to
> remember.
>
> (*She clears her throat, quickly checks her makeup.*) I
> know, I just know they are going to be wonderful assets
> to the new national recreational park which I am here

with you today to dedicate. In the next few years, there will be hundreds-of-pretty-pictures-of-these-colorful, uh, Indian natives, taken-here-in-this-neeyew park of ours, adding the excitement of a great outdoors vacation in the great American West to family photo albums in homes all across our land. Isn't-that-wonderful?

Applause cut short on tape, she fidgets nervously, smiles widely, hurries on with her speech.

The idea for this new park came directly from my husband, the pres-i-dent, and his assistant, the secretary of the interior. The three of us were having tea and ladyfingers in my sitting room in the family quarters of the White House, discussing ways to beautify America, and the secretary said to the pres-i-dent, "Mr. Pres-i-dent, I have a great idea. As you know sir, some of nature's most spectacular scenery is located right on many of the Indian reservations out West. Why don't we declare one of these reservations a national park?

(pause) It'll be a first." *(There is a stir in the Indian group.)* "The Indians get very little use of them anyway." The pres-i-dent said he thought it was a great idea, and time an entire Indian reservation be made a national park.

INDIAN

(with prop camera in hand, interrupting) Hey, First Lady, would you smile for me?

FIRST LADY

Why, why I'd be mighty happy to.

She strikes a lavish pose as the Indian clicks his shutter. A puff of smoke, sparks fly, the First Lady lets out a very ladylike scream. The Indians break up. Drilling sound, lights out, earth visuals.

69

8

_The lights reveal an isolated telephone booth at corner stage
left. Flashes of light pepper the distant background. A racing
siren wails faintly. A suggestion of the Washington Monument
can also be seen in the shadowy background. A man comes on,
wrapped in an Indian blanket, and anxiously enters the telephone booth._

SPY

> (_dialing furtively_) My God! Those damned Indians are
> crazier than the Afghans, the Congolese, the...

_His call number goes through, the sound of the telephone
clicking musically comes on tape._

VOICE

> Hell... o. White... uh, excuse me, I mean, thank you
> for calling, and how is the weather today?

SPY

> I'm not worried about the weather, pal. Who is this?
> Dwight? Gordon? Bob? Who? Which one of you guys am
> I talking with?

VOICE

> You... you know better than to refer directly to... uh,
> uh, the names of the innocent, oh, excuse me, I mean,
> certain individuals. Haven't we warned you enough
> times about doing that?

SPY

> Be serious. Who would dare listen in on a direct call to
> the White House? How could anybody be smart enough
> to tape, I mean tap, this call box? (_confusion_) Wait a
> minute. I'm not calling to argue about that, my friend,

you know I'm here on assignment. The Indians are going to blow the hell out of the Bureau of Indian Affairs building any time now. They have every kind of revolutionary armament and defensive device you can think of in that place. The entire joint is wired. I managed to infiltrate by wrapping a blanket around myself and putting on a braided wig. I look pretty convincing.

VOICE

What tribe were you passing for? Oh, never mind!

SPY

(*pleased*) As a matter of fact, I thought I looked like a Sioux (*pronounces it "Si-ox"*) or an Apache.

VOICE

And what is your reading of the situation? The boss has no time to devote to this matter just now. You know the election is just two days away. It cannot be blown. Do you understand that?

SPY

Yes, yes, yes! You know I understand. I'm just trying to be helpful, that's all. Helpful as long as you pay me, goddammit!

VOICE

Please, don't use profanity on this line!

SPY

Oh, excuse me, I forgot I was talking to the White . . . oh!

VOICE

Don't say it!

SPY

Okay! Okay! Now listen, the only way we can save the building and prevent a bloody massacre of all those Indians and head off an explosive situation which could turn into an extremely embarrassing mess for the administration in the eyes of the world is to . . .

VOICE

Yes, we're waiting.

SPY

Is to bribe 'em, buy 'em off! (*He looks around to see if he is being watched.*)

VOICE

How do you mean that? With beads, blankets, and whiskey?

SPY

No, hell no, dammit!

VOICE

Stop cursing, please!

SPY

No, no, we pay them cash, cold, hard cash. You know what that is, don't you? I know you do.

VOICE

How much?

SPY

I managed to do some figuring while I was inside the building. If my figures are correct, Indians are about two-thirds of one percent of the total population of the country, right? So, give them something like, uh, $66,500. Say to the press it's for travel expenses, to get the Indians back to their reservations. The public'll be impressed that even the poor old Indians are getting a little of the dole from Washington. Deliver the money to them in a briefcase. Or two if it all won't fit into one. Get it in and get out quick.

VOICE

(*indignant*) Hush money?

SPY

No, perfectly legal. Travel expenses. They're all government consultants. You can put it down as that.

VOICE

And yourself, how much for you?

SPY

My fee for this national security operation will be $250,000, in cold, cold, hard, hard cash, of course.

VOICE

(*disbelief*) Two hundred and fifty...

SPY

(*cutting him off*) You heard me, $250,000, in cold, hard cash!

VOICE

If we had to we could raise that, no problem. But we, we could use troops and tear gas to get those redskins out; why pay them? This is an unnecessary extravagance, highway robbery, plain old extortion.

SPY

Who says so?

VOICE

Well, you're getting more than the Indians will get, if this outrageously expensive transaction is approved.

SPY

This is dangerous work. I could have been scalped or killed if I had been caught in my disguise. And besides, the election will be in two days. You don't want a big bloody mess over here to foul things up, do you?

VOICE

Hang up now. I'll have to check this out with the Committee to Re... oh, pardon me, please. I need to consult my superiors. We'll be right back to you.

SPY

Don't take all night. This is an explosive situation over here. The specters of death and disaster are everywhere in the air. Have you ever been in the middle of a wild mob of hot-blooded warriors, buddy?

VOICE

Thank you so much for the weather report, Mr. Smith, uh, Jones.

Spy hangs up, looks again to see if he is watched. Phone rings intermittently.

SPY

This is Neptune. The fish are running.

VOICE

What kind of fish?

SPY

Red snappers.

VOICE

The word is go. We'll make the arrangements on this end to get the money to the Indians. It will look very proper. The public knows how money-happy all Indians are, so miserable and poor, and our most isolated minority. They'll do anything to get their hands on some. Giving them money is a wonderful way to show them and the voters how much this administration cares. How do we get yours to you?

SPY

The usual way.

VOICE

Thank you for this weather report.

SPY

Sure, any time.

He hangs up, steps outside the booth, is showered with money. Drilling sound, earth visuals. Lights out.

74

9

The performing group lines up in a choreographed pattern as the piano begins "Pass That Peace Pipe."[1] *Between each of the stanzas of the song, delivered as a wild production number, an actor wearing a bull's head is spotlighted with a pretty girl in pigtails, who reads from a giant roll of toilet tissue. The bull also holds a roll, and unwinds enough tissue to wipe his behind each time a treaty is called out.*

CHORUS

IF YOUR TEMPER'S GETTIN' THE TOP HAND
ALL YOU GOTTA DO IS JUST STOP AND
PASS THAT PEACE PIPE AND BURY THAT HATCHET
LIKE THE CHOCTAWS, CHICKASAWS, CHATTAHOOCHIES,
CHIPPEWAS DO!

GIRL

(leading the bull to front of stage)
THE TREATY OF ATOKA!
(action)
THE TREATY OF NEW ECHOTA!
(action)
THE TREATY OF DANCING RABBIT CREEK.
(action)
THE TREATY OF 1851.
(action)

CHORUS

IF YOU'RE FEELIN' MAD AS A WET HEN
MAD AS YOU CAN POSSIBLY GET, THEN

[1]"Pass That Peace Pipe and Bury That Hatchet" by Roger Edens, Hugh Martin, and Ralph Blane. Copyright © 1943, 1947 by Robbins Music Corporation. Copyright renewed. Chappell & Co., Inc., owner of publication and mechanical rights. International copyright secured. ALL RIGHTS RESERVED. Used by permission.

PASS THAT PEACE PIPE AND BURY THAT TOMAHAWK
LIKE THOSE CHICHIMECS, CHEROKEES, CHEPULTEPECS,
TOO!

GIRL

THE TREATY OF MEDICINE LODGE CREEK!
(*action*)
THE TREATY OF PORT ELLIOTT!
(*action*)
THE TREATY OF THE LITTLE ARKANSAS!
(*action*)
THE TREATY OF FORT WISE!
(*action*)

CHORUS

DON'T BE CRANKY, TRY TO USE A LITTLE RESTRAINT
FOLD THAT HANKY, AND WIPE OFF ALL OF THAT
   WAR PAINT!
AND IF YOU FIND YOURSELF IN A FURY, BE YOUR
   OWN JUDGE AND YOUR OWN JURY!
PASS THAT PEACE PIPE AND BURY THAT HATCHET
LIKE THE CHOCTAWS, CHICKASAWS, CHATTAHOOCHIES,
CHIPPEWAS, DO!

GIRL

THE TREATY OF FORT LARAMIE!
(*action*)
THE TREATY OF MEDICINE LODGE!
(*action*)
THE TREATY OF FORT KLAMATH!
(*action*)
AND THE TREATY OF POINT NO POINT!
(*action*)

CHORUS

WRITE THAT APOLOGY, AND DISPATCH IT,
WHEN YOU'VE QUARRELED, IT'S BETTER TO PATCH IT.
PASS THAT PEACE PIPE AND BURY THAT HATCHET

LIKE THE CHOCTAWS, CHICKASAWS, CHATTAHOOCHIES, CHIPPEWAS,
AND THOSE CHICHIMECS, CHEROKEES, CHEPULTEPECS,
AND THOSE CHICUTIMEES, CHEPECHETS AND CHICAPEES,
CHO-CHOS, CHANGOS, CHATTANOOGAS, CHEECAROWS, DO!

Drilling sound, earth visuals, lights

10

The choreography and music for this Wild West Show sequence provides the performing group members wide latitude for clowning. A girl in flimsy costume runs onstage with a show card to announce each scene. (The show cards will read: WILD APACHES; INDIAN COUNCIL OF WAR; LOVELY WHITE MAIDEN; SCALP DANCE; *and* TRIUMPH OF THE WHITES.*) The Indians wear fake war bonnets, ride stick horses and yelp war whoops.*

ANNOUNCER'S VOICE
(*on tape*) COMING SOON! COMING SOON! TO THE OLYMPIC THEATER! DIRECTLY FROM THEIR HOMES IN THE WILD, WILD WEST!! THE WI—LD APACHES OF ARIZONA!

(*music up, Indians ride onstage.*) Stalwart Braves and Squaws, Without Doubt the Finest Specimens of the Aborigines Ever Seen in this City in a Live Show of this Kind!

THIS ENTERTAINMENT WILL CONSIST OF A SERIES OF STIRRING TABLEAUX, INTENSELY AND ACCURATELY ILLUSTRATIVE OF INDIAN MODES AND CUSTOMS, NEVER BEFORE SO FAITHFULLY SET FORTH!!

(music up)
See Unbelievable, Breathtaking Scenes
Of Thrilling Hand-To-Hand Combat.
A True-To-Life Indian Council of War!
Featuring Speeches in the Actual Indian Tongues,
By the Noted Chiefs and Braves.
The Breaking of the Arrow!

(music up)
An original, authentic WAAARRR DANCE!

Music and drumming create transition: all performers exit for entrance of Lovely White Maiden.

See the Lovely White Maiden!
The surprise!
The chase!
The taking of the scalp!
A Savage, Brutal SCALP DANCE!
THE TRIUMPH OF THE WHITES!

Loud drumbeat for shotgun blast ends scalp dance and knocks the Indians dead on stage floor.

These, as well as many other fascinating true-to-life scenes of this vanishing specimen of primitive mankind.

Piano now fading. Show-card girl tiptoes among the Indian bodies with her final card.

Special matinees of this fantastic spectacle will be given on Saturdays and Sundays, as well as all national and civic holidays.

Show-card girl flits off. With the bodies on the floor, the drilling sound and earth slides are now more intense than

Photograph by Chris Spotted Eagle

before. In an instant they change to rifle fire and vistas of the terrain around Wounded Knee, South Dakota. The visuals stop on a single picture of a marshal peering through a rifle scope that is aimed toward the performers and the audience.

11

The performing group members now rise from the floor and form a semicircle around the drummer, who is bare-chested. He drums and sings The AIM Song, building to a spirited pitch. A single rifle shot rings out and the drummer falls forward, his body taut, glistening in the lights. The helicopters, armored cars, and more gunfire are heard. The picture of the marshal switches to a sequence of action shots of the siege of Wounded Knee in 1973.

MARSHAL'S VOICE
> (*mixed with sounds of siege on tape*) May I please have your attention! I am the United States District Marshal from Rapid City, and I am at the head of a force of 500 federal officers and deputies. We have the entire area surrounded. You cannot escape.

The performers lift the drummer's body, raise it above their heads, and begin a slow procession offstage.

> It is my duty to inform you that you are all under arrest on the charge of unlawfully trespassing on private property. Warrants for your arrest have been issued in federal district court. I must caution all of you not to make any sudden moves. We are armed and are prepared to take any necessary defensive action. All of you who do not surrender without resistance are hereby warned that additional charges will be filed against you for resisting arrest.
> Your hands must be held high above your heads until the handcuffs are placed on you.
> Again, I warn you, do not make any sudden moves.

Your cooperation will help to speed this procedure. Move forward, stay at absolute arms length.

The siege visuals end as the performing group files back on the darkened stage in a funeral procession, led by a drummer who sounds a single heavy beat. The men carry the body of the dead drummer covered by a star blanket. A series of visuals showing the hands of the performing group members being handcuffed are projected as they file off. Then, one by one, they return to the stage, handcuffed, with their arms raised above their heads. The narrator steps to the front of the group.

NARRATOR

We move on. To a courtroom in Rapid City, South Dakota. To a courtroom in Sioux Falls, Iowa.

PERFORMER

(Moving out from the group, he thrusts his hands toward audience.) I am Pawnee.

NARRATOR

We move on.

PERFORMER

(repeating the action) I am Creek.

NARRATOR

Back to our homes, our people.

PERFORMER

I am Winnebago.

NARRATOR

We move on.

PERFORLMER

I am Sioux.

NARRATOR

To the land.

PERFORMER
I am Apache.

NARRATOR
To the sky.

PERFORMER
I am Ojibwa.

The lights dim as the apparition of the Indian face again appears on the stage backside and moves slowly around the playing area.

VOICE OF SPANISH SAILOR
(*on tape*) ¡Capitan! ¡Capitan! ¡Dios mio! ¡Muchas gracias! ¡Madre mia! ¡Los indios! ¡Los indios! ¡India! ¡Ellos son los indios!

NARRATOR
(*very compassionately*) I am . . . NOT GUILTY!

Lights fade slowly. Performing group exits.

END

49

49

---

49 was first performed by the Native American Theater Ensemble at Oklahoma City University on January 10, 1975, with the following cast:

NIGHT WALKER	Gerald Bruce Miller
SINGING MAN	Jim Box
WEAVING WOMAN	Regina Box
BTY	Joe Harjo
GIRL	Glenda Fields
ALL OTHERS	Maggie Geiogamah, Joe Madrano, Bonnie Baker, Clarence Toledo, and Wauhilla Doonkeen.

Directed by Hanay Geiogamah
Set designed by Gerald Bruce Miller
Lighting by Debra Jefferson Fedyk
Choreography by Gerald Bruce Miller and Jim Box
Musical arrangements by Clarence Toledo
Special art by Jim Box

The People of the Play

NIGHT WALKER, ceremonial leader of the tribe, can be any
   age
BALLADEER, a young Indian singer of today
MEMBERS OF THE 49 GROUP
HIGHWAY PATROLMAN
SPIRITS
YOUNG PEOPLE OF THE TRIBE
YOUNG DUDE BY THE CAR
SINGING MAN; BOY AND GIRL OF THE TRIBE
WEAVING WOMAN; GIRLS OF THE TRIBE
YOUTHS IN CAR: GIRL DRIVER; PASSENGERS; GIRL IN BACK
   SEAT
OLD LADY VISITOR FROM FAR AWAY
CHIEFS
YOUNG WARRIORS
PEOPLE OF THE TRIBE
LEAD SINGERS AND DRUMMERS OF THE 49
TWO FIGHTING DUDES AND THEIR GIRLFRIENDS
49 LEAD MAN

Setting: A ceremonial ground circa 1885 and the same ceremonial ground in the present.

Music and Songs of the Play[1]

An experienced traditional drummer (or drummers), willing to experiment with varied rhythms, must attend all rehearsals to assist in developing the music for the production and to devise a pattern of drum rhythms that can extend throughout the entire performance at varied tempos and levels to provide a taut structure for the play. The music can employ bells, rattles, ratchets, bull-roarers, Apache violins, flutes, whistles, various sizes of drums, piano, and guitars.

[1]Music and lyrics for 49 copyrighted 1975 by Hanay Geiogamah and Jim Pepper.

Author's Note

A 49 celebration usually begins about midnight or just after, when the more formal activities of the powwow or Indian fair or tribal celebration are over. There is a loosely structured pattern of time and movement in the formation of a 49 congregation. Forty-nines always take place at night; really good ones go on until sunrise and after. More young people are involved than older ones, and thus the scene is charged with the energy of hundreds of youths. A typical timetable for a 49 is as follows:

Midnight—gradual formation; 1 A.M.—singing and dancing begin; 2 A.M.—singing and dancing intensify, fringe activities well underway; 3 A.M.—singing still strong, dancing dropping off, fringe activities at zenith, traffic jams, first police efforts at raids; 4 A.M.—singing sporadic, fights, all important contacts made, police seriously threaten periphery of 49; 5 A.M.—singing stops, thin groupings, car activities, final effort to "snag"; 6 A.M.—sunup, stragglers, efforts to start stalled cars, diehards gradually depart the scene.

In a memorandum to the members of the Native American Theater Ensemble before beginning rehearsals for the show, I made these comments about the specialness of 49'ing:

—While taking part in a 49, young Indians are in an extremely heightened state of awareness of their "Indianness."

—They achieve, with amazing rapidity and with a minimum of friction, a group conviviality that is intertribal.

—They flirt with the dangers of police harrassment and arrest, jailing, automobile accidents, and injuries from fighting.

—They sing and dance their own versions of Indian songs with more earnestness, sensitivity, and good humor than they do at any other time (some do not sing and dance at all except during 49s).

Given the difficult circumstances that often prevent so many Indians from taking any meaningful part in tribal ceremonies, they find in the 49 not only an emotional release but also a means of expressing thoughts and attitudes difficult to articulate under less stimulating conditions.

In the play the figure of the shaman Night Walker creates the tie between the young people's past and their present and future. He can move supernaturally between both eras and speak directly to both generations. Night Walker is probably a little disappointed that nothing more solid and serious than 49 has emerged for the young Indians, but he is always optimistic, never without hope. His movements and statements provide the text with what I would describe as a combination of restraint and release, turbulence and repose.

More than anything else I wanted the young people to be affirmative in the face of despair and unreasoning force. I had an instinct to minimize the negative and sought to do this even though much of the action is essentially negative. Let that be, I said, and let the principal focus fall on the young people's spirit, the sinews of strength that hold all of them together, that keep them going, that provide their energy.

The self-realization comes about largely through nonverbal means. Instead of using the kind of abuse ("Pigs!") that accomplishes nothing, they move smoothly to form the human barricade in the final scene as if by a shared and positive instinct. Their defiance is strong, but calm and totally controlled. They feel and know what they should do, and the power of this understanding is expressed in the body formation that is the "beautiful bird" that Night Walker sees flying.

Scene 1

A single light reveals a dance area of tightly packed earth with trees, grass, and bushes growing alongside. There are brush arbors in the background, and a roadway extends out of the area. A high embankment rises above the roadway, and more trees are in back of this. Other lights start to come up with the Ute Flute Calling Melody, which floats through the night air. The lights progressively illumine other corners of this ceremonial area, a much-used site with a long history of many tribespeople coming and going. Night Walker enters slowly, moves around the area with poise and dignity, gesturing expansively.

NIGHT WALKER
Greetings. Hello. Good day to you.
Greetings. Hello. Good day to you.

I, Night Walker, spiritual leader of the tribe, our people, speak to all of the young people of the tribe, our people.

Will you hear my voice?
Will you hear my voice?

Hear me, Night Walker. I have a thing of very strong purpose to say to you. It is a thing of deepest concern for the tribe, our people.

I ask all of the young men and women of the tribe, our people, to come to the ceremonial circle, to our people's arbor, so that I may speak with you.

I will pray for all of you there. I will tell you of this
purpose.

(*now with more urgency*)

The tribe, our people, need you!
The tribe, our people, need you!

(*moving off now*)

Thank you.

Thank you.

The flute melody fades as the lights dim out.

Scene 2

---

*A sudden, jagged crackle of a two-way police radio breaks the
calm. The lights on the set are shifting gently, magically.*

PATROL VOICE 1
Unit 9? Unit 9? This is Unit 4. Do you read me?

PATROL VOICE 2
I read you, Unit 4.

PATROL VOICE 1
I'm sittin' solid three miles west, two miles north of the
Apache Y.

PATROL VOICE 2
Ain't seen none yet. City says they're a-drivin' around
town like ants. Hunnerds of 'em. More'n all week. Lot of
'em from out of town. It always gets kind-ee wild t'ord
the end of this fair, but this year seems wilder than ever.

PATROL VOICE 1
Yep, it's perty wild. Got sixty-five of 'em in the county

jail and all filled up in the city. Ever damn one of 'em's under age. Can't pay their fines. We'll get us a bunch more of 'em tonight, I betcha.

PATROL VOICE 2

I have an idee they'll be a-headin' for the old Whitehorse Road tonight. They claim that lil' dance ground out there's Indian property and that no law officers can trespass or arrest a Indian there.

PATROL VOICE 1

Trespass my ass. (*He laughs.*)

PATROL VOICE 2

(*with surprise*) Hey! Boy! One just went by . . . loaded down! Left front out. I'm a-following.

A spotlight locates the Balladeer. A single car headlight hits the roadway directly in a flash as lights reveal youths packed into a car, a mixed lot, obviously en route to a 49.

BALLADEER

COME ON, DANCE 49, HONEY
COME ON, DANCE WITH ME
COME ON, DANCE 49, HONEY
COME ON, DANCE WITH ME.

TEACH YOU HOW TO SING TURTLE SONG, HONEY
SHOW YOU HOW TO DANCE WITH ME
TEACH YOU HOW TO SING TURTLE SONG, HONEY
SHOW YOU HOW TO DANCE WITH ME.

I GOT A DRUM
LET'S MAKE A SONG
I'LL SING TO YOU, HONEY
ALL NIGHT LONG.

TAKE YOU DOWN TO ANADARKO WITH ME, HONEY
TAKE YOU OUT TO TAHLEQUAH

UP TO THE OSAGE COUNTRY FOR THE POWWOWS
HONEY COME ON BLAZE WITH ME
HONEY COME ON BLAZE WITH ME.

COME ON DANCE 49, HONEY
COME ON SING WITH ME
COME ON DANCE 49, HONEY
COME ON, BE WITH ME.
(*light out on Balladeer.*)

YOUTH IN CAR
(*looking back*) Damn cops!

The 49 group mimes the car as they careen around the environment, the lights following their movements. The Balladeer moves about, following their progress, and begins to sing accompaniment as the police give chase with red lights flashing.

BALLADEER
THEY DON'T KNOW WHY THOSE DAMNED PATROLS
WON'T LEAVE 'EM ALONE
HO WAY YAW HEY YEY
THEY DON'T KNOW WHY THOSE DAMNED PATROLS
WON'T LEAVE 'EM ALONE
HOWAY YAW HEY
HO WAY YAW HEY YEY EY YO!

THEY WANT TO TAKE 'EM ALL TO JAIL
HO WAY YAW HEY
HO WAY YAW HEY YEY
LOCK 'EM UP
GIVE 'EM HELL
HO WAY YAW HEY
HO WAY YAW HEY YEY EY YO.

DIS/OR/DER/LY AND DRUNK/EN/NESS
HO WAY YAW HEY

HO WAY YAW HEY YEY
THIRTY DAYS!
HO WAY YAW HEY
HO WAY
HO WAY
HO WAY YAW HEY YEY EY YO!

BUT THEY CAN ALL GO STRAIGHT TO HELL!
HO WAY YAW HEY
HO WAY YAW HEY YEY
STRAIGHT TO HELL!
HO WAY YAW HEY
HO WAY
HO WAY
HO WAY YAW HEY YEY EY YO!

The 49 group dive for cover in the underbrush to escape the police and take positions of hiding. A police car search-light scans the terrain slowly, fades out.

Scene 3

Lights reveal Night Walker, whose body is making the motions of a journey through rugged terrain. Odd flashes of light illuminate his progress, which is being observed by masks and faces of humans and animals. The 49 group are in their hiding positions throughout the scene. Night Walker reaches a clearing, composes himself, and delivers a prayer that is directed as much to himself as to the power spirits.

NIGHT WALKER
I heed as unto those I call.
I heed as unto those I call.
Send to me thy potent aid.

Help us, the tribe, our people, oh, holy place around. Help us, our friends, our brothers and sisters. We heed as unto thee we call.

I come to visit with my brothers and sisters. Will you hear my voice?

Will you hear my voice? The voice of a friend who has honor and respect deep in his heart for you?

I am the oldest man of the tribe, our people. You, my brothers and sisters, have given me this honor of life.

The masks and faces and supernatural activities become larger.

You know my voice. We sing together. You were at my birth. You know my father. You know my father's father, and you know his father. You are kind and generous to all of us, the tribe, our people.

Will I sing for you now? I will tell you a story of a bear who comes to watch the dancing of the tribe, our people. (*pause*) Some of the people say the bear is learning our songs.

I have brought food for my friends. I will make a meal for us. I will make a fire. I will spread my blankets.

He does these things.

I have tobacco with me. I is good tobacco.

I have sage that was brought to the tribe our people from a place far away from our home. I will burn it for you.

He waits, then lights the sage.

I saw a young man and a young girl of the tribe our

96

people the other day. (*pause*) They both were smiling and happy. I looked at them for a long time. I watched them walk about. I saw in their smiles the signs of a family of wonderful hunters and weavers.

I had a feeling to speak with them, but I... did... not.

The faces move closer.

The faces of these two young ones appear before me now. I bring their smiles here for my friends to see.

I am made sad... by... these smiles. My friends!

I am the youngest man of the tribe, our people. You, my brothers and sisters have given me this honor.

Haw!
Haw!
I know.
I hope.
I pray.

He has established communication.

I dream.
I smile.
I do.
Haw!
I know the smiles.
I see.
I am the oldest man of the tribe. Haw! Haw!
The young ones' smiles are my smiles.
It is I who am smiling.
I am the girl.
I am the boy.

Yes.
They will both know that I am they.

A longer pause. A jew's harp and Apache violin[2] *are heard.*

The men chiefs of the tribe, our people, do not look to me when they talk with me of the things that concern the good of the tribe, our people.

They do not tell me all that they want me to know.

When they return to the tribe, our people, after fighting with the enemies, I must talk more and more to Brother Death.

I must ask Brother Death . . . to . . . take the spirits . . . of the young men . . . who have stopped living . . . with us.

Haw! I wait.
Haw!
I see.
I see. Brother Death sees too. How long? How far?

He lights more sage, then the young people begin, with soft voices, the Sioux Medicine Chant, and sing it as a counterpoint to Night Walker's prayer.

I have come here for the young man whose smiles I see.
I have come here for the young woman, who is so pretty.
I have come here for the warrior chiefs who will not look at me.
I am the oldest man of the tribe.
I have come here as two smiles who cannot see into the darkness that I see, gathering ahead on our road.

[2]An Apache violin is a one-string instrument that produces a monotone similar to a running single note repeated on a violin.

Must Brother Death direct their eyes? (*very firmly*)

Must all life be taken from us?
My friends know.

I do not know about the smiling faces of the young man and the young woman of the tribe, our people.

I do not know how long the young people will know the smell of the sage and the cedar.

I sing. Will they sing? Many beautiful songs?
I dance. How will they know to dance?
I make pictures of color. Will they see this beauty?

I conduct the ceremonies of our journey. Which one of them will follow me to lead?

I heal my sister's child. Will they know the medicine of the tribe, our people?

I have learned the way of Brother Winter and I talk with our brothers in the grass and trees and in the sky. Will they know these friends?

I am the oldest man of the tribe, our people, and I give help to my brothers and sisters in our journey.

The answer is completed.

They will hear my voice. They will hear your voices. They will look to me. They will look to you.

We live a very long time. They will live a very long time. I am not afraid. I will not stop walking. I will not stop singing. I will not stop dancing. I will talk to all of my friends for a very long time. We will walk through the dark that *has* passed us, the tribe, our people. A-ho! A-ho, pah-bes. A-ho.

We will live and walk together for a long time. All of us will live and walk together for a long time.

He bows deeply and remains in the position as the Sioux Medicine Chant builds, then fades to end the scene. His exit is like a disappearance.

Scene 4

In the darkness a youth strikes a match and draws it slowly toward his face, illuminating his features until he whistles softly, blowing it out.

Other matches and whistles begin to dot the scene.

The 49 group one by one come out of their hiding positions and begin circling in an effort to find each other.

The Water-whistles Song is heard as this night ballet unfolds.

They find their friends and partners, stand together in small groups, check the night air for a feeling of safety.

When the group has re-formed, the song, which has no words, ends. All lights go to a blue shading to complete the scene.

Scene 5

The dance arena is dimly lit, quiet. Car lights appear moving on in the distance. Sounds of car motors are heard mixed with sounds of the night. Other lights rise slowly, gently; deep patches of color flow through the setting to contrast with the night sky. The images of a caravan of Indian cars come into focus. Dust, noise, a sense of gathering. Flutes, bells are heard as members of the 49 group filter into the area of the dance ground. The colors of the lights now begin to look dazzling. The elation of the participants grows as they claim the area as their own for the 49. Night Walker sits above the action, observing calmly. Two youths enter with a dance drum and pause in the circle center. A third youth lights a match to heat the head of the drum for tuning. The 49 Balladeer appears atop the embankment and a drum roll echoes as he begins to sing.

BALLADEER

> YAH HEY YAAH
> YAH HEY YAAH
> HEY EY YAH EY YA HO
> EY YAH HEY
> YAH EY YAH HEY YEY
> YAH EY YAH HO
> EY YAH HEY
> YAH EY YAH HO
> EY YAH HEY
> EY YAH HEY
> EY YO
> YA KA MA DA 49!

He repeats the vocables, then the 49 group join in Ya-ka-mada 49 and dance with powerful drive. When the singing ends, the drumming rolls to a stop with whooping and yelling, begins again immediately with another drum roll, and the Balladeer leads off another song.

BALLADEER

> JUST WHEN WE GET TOGETHER, SWEETHEART
> WE'LL SING AND DANCE ALL NIGHT

AND THEN WE'LL ROCK TO THE 49
HEY O YAH HO EY YAH HEY EY YAH HEY YO!

The 49, with its restless movements, its shifting images and special sounds, comes fully to life.

PATROL VOICE 1
(*as 49 activities surge*) This is Unit 4. Unit 4 to Units 5, 6, 7, and 8. Come in , Units 5, 6, 7, and 8. Do you read me? (*They check in.*) Unit 9 reports fifty or more cars in the area of the old Whitehorse Road, nine mile west, two mile north. Repeat, 49's starting on the old Whitehorse Road, nine mile west, two mile north. Red '64 Chevy four-door sedan parked on the westbound side about a mile up from the turn-off, abandoned there by twelve to fourteen Indian youths. Nine says more cars're comin' in from the west by a off-county road line. Units 5, 6, 7, 8, advise to proceed to the area. Call check thirty minutes. Repeat, call check thirty minutes. Over.

The drumbeat continues as the lights fade slowly on youths moving in and out of the round dance.

Scene 6

The young people of the tribe are assembled to hear Night Walker. Parents and relatives may be watching at a distance. Note: The young tribal members are costumed for an earlier era, and they conduct themselves in the manner of students of Night Walker.

NIGHT WALKER
(*in full command*)
I tell you of things I know.

I tell you of things I see.
I tell you to prepare you
For all that is coming.
For a loss
That will be like death to our people.

Consternation among the young people; he lets them settle down.

Soon, we will live in a different land.
I cannot see this place.

Soon, we will be forced from our arbor.

Soon, the singing will stop.
Soon, there will be no dancing.
The pipe will not burn.
We will forget our stories.
We will not meet our friends.

Harsh red lights reveal a field littered with buffalo skeletons and bones. These images intermingle with the shadows of the young people.

Soon, we will not have the things that make our way the way we know.
Soon, all our hearts will feel this pain.

Soon, the tribe, our people, will be told that we cannot do anything they do not want us to do.

Soon, we will sit in the grass and wonder where we are going.

Soon, we will close our eyes to not see what will be before them.

You will ask yourselves who you are.

Photograph by Fred Marvel

If I knew why this must be I would tell you.

You will know.

The death images fade.

YOUNG PEOPLE
(*in unison*) We will follow you, grandfather, you show us
the way.

The Pollen Road melody is heard in the distance.

NIGHT WALKER
Sing with me. I will lead you.
Dance along with me. I will show you the steps.
Know how we came to this place.
Know the stories of our way.
Know the way I know, and I will follow you.
We will follow you.
You will lead.
Do not be afraid to make new songs.

YOUNG PEOPLE
We will walk by you
Through times of suffering and sorrow
To a life for us that will be new.

NIGHT WALKER
You must lead our clan
To a time of understanding
When a man will not hurt a man
By killing his way of living.

YOUNG PEOPLE
We move out onto the plain.
We begin this journey.
We will endure the pain.
We take the pipe, the tipi.

NIGHT WALKER
    I pray for you.
    I sing for you.
    I smoke for you.
    I give to you
    These things.
    You give them life.

He distributes a drum, a fan, feathers. The Pollen Road melody and chant intensify. The drumbeat builds to a sharp pitch, then rolls down.

YOUNG PEOPLE
    HEY AH NAH HEY NAY
    HEY AH NAH HEY NAY
    HEY AH NAH HEY NAY
    HEY AH NAH HEY NAY OH

    WALKING TO THE EAST
    EVERYTHING IS BEAUTIFUL
    WALKING TO THE WEST
    EVERYTHING IS BEAUTIFUL
    WALKING TO THE NORTH
    EVERYTHING IS BEAUTIFUL
    WALKING TO THE SOUTH
    EVERYTHING IS BEAUTIFUL

    HEY AH NAH HEY NAY
    HEY AH NAH HEY NAY
    HEY AH NAH HEY NAY
    HEY AH NAH HEY NAY OH

    WALKING DOWN THAT POLLEN ROAD
    EVERYTHING IS BEAUTIFUL
    WALKING DOWN THAT POLLEN ROAD
    EVERYTHING IS BEAUTIFUL

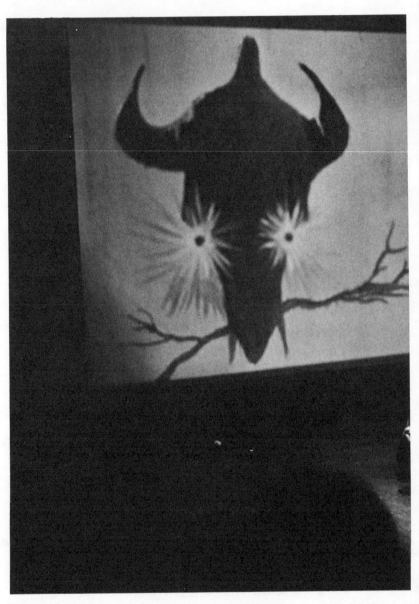

Photograph by Fred Marvel

HEY AH NAH HEY NAY
HEY AH NAH HEY NAY
HEY AH NAH HEY NAY OH

They move about the environment, then form a circle and raise their faces upward.

PATROL VOICE 1
> Unit 4? Unit 4? Come in, Unit 4. This is Unit 6. Unit 6. Do you read me? Over.

PATROL VOICE 2
> This is Unit 4. I read you, Unit 6.

PATROL VOICE 1
> I'm sittin' solid a mile back east of the Whitehorse turn-off. There's no activity this side of 62. Nothing north either. Over.

PATROL VOICE 2
> Sit solid, Unit 6. I'd say there's more'n 300 cars down in there now. Five, 7, 8, and 9'll have to go in with us. Over.

PATROL VOICE 1
> Roger. Sittin' solid. You give the call. Over.

Lights fade on the circle of young people.

Scene 7

Several youths surround the front of one of the cars. The 49 movements form a low-key background. A seventeen- or eighteen-year-old holds the center of attention in the group. He speaks solo.

YOUTH
> (*to one of group*) Hey, guy, how many you think's here?

110

'Bout two thousand! Geeyall, heey!
I wonder how many of 'em's snaggin'! Geeyall!
I'll, uh, I'll break 'em all up with a good one, aaah!
Which one can ya'll sing? A good one, heeey!
I wanna' lead a really good one, geeyall.
Which one? I need practice before I hit, geeyall. I can
lead good, guy.
Which one?
Birdlegs?
Birdlegs? Geeyall, a old one.

He pretends to drum on the car hood. Others in the group are in a playful mood too.

YOUTH
Who's gonna' second me? Which one of you, geeyall?
Birdlegs, a old one. Birdlegs Special. Geeyall!

He play-drums again on the car hood, realizing he is losing the group's attention.

YOUTH
(*suddenly, with wide grin and delight*) KAY TASS AH YOK
AH ME DAH QUASSS! AAAHHHH!. GEEEYALLL!

Laughter from the group.

YOUTH
(still happy) Yeah, it's a old one. I know it. Geeeyalll!

Lights transfer to dancers, then dim out.

Scene 8

Night Walker is speaking to a group of the young tribespeople underneath the arbor. The Singing Man is instructing a sec-

*ond group around a large drum, and some young girls listen to
Weaving Woman, who sits beside a weaving loom. Sounds of
camp life and its activities are heard in the background.*

SINGING MAN
Our people have had these gifts since before our long
journey here. The mother gave the tribe, our people,
this drum. For us its sound is the sound of her heart
beating with life.

*He describes the flute, the bells, and the rattles. This is done
in mime; none of his words are heard by the audience. He then
gives the drumsticks to a boy and a girl, and they slowly begin
to beat a rhythm.*

BOY
(*shyly, lightening the beat*) A song came to me the other
day when I was by the river. It is a short song, about a
turtle.

SINGING MAN
Turtles are my good friends. They have fun at night
when their other friends are sleeping. Sing your song.

BOY
(*halting*) AH NAH HEY MAH... (*He stops, looks at the
girl, nudges her to join.*) She knows it too. I taught her.

SINGING MAN
Good. Sing the turtle song. I'll sing it with you, if you
teach me.

BOY AND GIRL
AH NAH HEY MAH/KONE KEEN GYA HON SAY/MYONG YAH
HEY/PEENG PONE GYA/EY YAH HEY EY YAH HEY EY YO.

SINGING MAN
If the turtle can give you such a song, you can find many
more beautiful ones almost everywhere you look, yes?

Photograph by Fred Marvel

GIRL
  We have a song that we sing to each other.

SINGING MAN
  My woman has found many songs for me. I sing for her
  by the campfire at night.
  (*He beats the drum softly, outlining a song.*) Will you
  sing for me the song you have for each other?

BOY
  It is a good song, but it is not finished yet.

SINGING MAN
  I know many songs which are not finished. They are still
  songs. Sing.

BOY
  I will finish the song now. Will you help me? I want to
  take this song with me to the new place where we will
  live.

*The Singing Man looks to Night Walker, who looks down at
the scene.*

SINGING MAN
  Yes. Sing.

BOY
  If you will drum.

SINGING MAN
  You drum. You will feel your song more if you do.

*The boy adds vocables to his words, The Kiowa Turtle Song,
sings it through, then repeats it in full. The Singing Man joins
him.*

ENTIRE GROUP
  AH NAH HEY MAH
  KONE KEEN
  GYA HON SAY
  MYONG YAH HEY

PEENG PONE GYA
EY YAH HEY
EY YAH HEY EY YO.

SINGING MAN

Our music is everywhere. You can find it wherever you look. It can find you too. When a song comes to you, learn it. Learn it and give it to others. And do not forget to thank the turtle for his song, or your hearts for their music. Always show that you are thankful for the gift of music. It is a wonderful blessing. The people will always have songs if... you... sing.

Lights transfer to the weaving circle.

WEAVING WOMAN

(*as she displays a beautiful blanket*) I have had this design since my mother gave it to me many years ago. She took the pattern from the red ants as they make their way. She wove some of her own hair into the design so that a part of her could be with the blanket as long as the blanket lives.

FIRST GIRL

Will... I keep... my design... for my children and for their children?

WEAVING WOMAN

It will be yours, and theirs, and ours, if you make it so beautiful that nobody else can duplicate its beauty. The tribe will be honored for the beauty you create.

SECOND GIRL

(*hesitantly*) But... our way... is... is ... changing. How will we make our designs live in the blankets if we have no ... sheep to give us wool for the loom?

WEAVING WOMAN

(*after a pause*) A design can live and grow for many years before it is placed on the loom. You can always see it ... when you close your eyes. You can change the colors, line them up in other patterns. You can have many different designs. They will be happy to wait if you promise them that you will keep them until there is ... wool ... for the ... looms.

A single spot illuminates the blanket; all other lights down soft.

PATROL VOICE 1
Seven and eight, do you read me?
PATROL VOICE 2
Seven reads.
PATROL VOICE 3
Eight reads.
PATROL VOICE 1
Sittin' solid.
PATROL VOICE 2
Sittin' solid.
PATROL VOICE 3
Sittin' solid.

The spot fades slowly on the blanket, then out.

Scene 9

The lights isolate a group of eight youths packed tightly into a small car, searching for the 49. Some of them show the effects of being buzzed and high. The girl driving the car is very eager to reach the scene. A drumbeat paces the scene and builds steadily to the climax.

DRIVER
Dammit. I thought they all went to T-Bird Hill.

YOUTH
> The law's probably got there first.

DRIVER
> Damn, we're 'bout outa gas.

GIRL IN BACK SEAT
> Well, hell, slow down! You're goin' too fast. We'll get there.

DRIVER
> We got enough to get to Moonlight.

GIRL IN BACK SEAT
> Well, slow down.

The driver switches on the car radio, flips stations, and lights a cigarette as others in the car shift, giggle, embrace.

DRIVER
> How far is Moonlight from T-Bird?

YOUTH
> Forty-nine thousand miles! Aaiiee. (*laughter from all*)

GIRL
> Dammit, slow down. You don't even know where you're goin'!

DRIVER
> I'm not goin' too fast. I wanna' get there. I gotta' find you-know-who before he finds you-know-who.

GIRL
> Aw, he'll be there. Be careful.

DRIVER
> (*approaching a turn in the road*) Which way do I turn? Left?

YOUTH
> Yeah, left, then straight for 'bout six miles.

DRIVER
> (*adjusting after turning*) Oh, damn, it's almost two. He's probably already snagged that damned ugly thing.

She accelerates; others shift places, become tense.

YOUTH

> (*to driver*) It's only 'bout four more miles. You gotta turn
> right after that sign on that mile corner road. You better
> slow down a little bit, cops might be parked down that
> way.

GIRL

> Yeah, slow down!

DRIVER

> I'm all right, I'm drivin' okay.

*Silence. All in the group are looking directly ahead, watching
for the point to turn. Other girls adjust their hair, and so
forth.*

YOUTH

> We're coming to that turn-off road. 'Bout 'nother mile.

DRIVER

> Tell me before we get there.

*(She accelerates again, and the passengers sit up rigidly in
response.)*

DRIVER

> I bet he's got in a big fight.

GIRL

> (*nervous*) Don't go so fast! That turn's right up there.
> You're gonna' miss it.

DRIVER

> No, I won't.

YOUTH

> There it is, right up there. Slow down! It's right there.

DRIVER

> (*shifting down*) I see it.

GIRL

> Slow down!

There are sounds of grinding gears and squealing tires and all in the car brace for the turn.

DRIVER

 (*turning steering wheel wildly without direction*) Dammit! I can't see that damn road!

GIRL

 (*terror in her voice*) Oh, damn you, stop! We're gonna' wreck!

Others scream as the car goes out of control, sending their bodies flying over the seats. The lights flash in lurches. Crash sounds. Silence. A single shaft of light falls on the Balladeer, who stands atop the embankment, looking first down to the scene, then up and away from it.

BALLADEER

 OH, YES, I LOVE YOU HONEY
 I DON'T CARE IF YOU'RE MARRIED SIXTEEN TIMES
 I STILL LOVE YOU
 I'LL GET YOU YET
 WHEE YAH HI, WHEE YAH HI UH YO!
 OH, YES, I LOVE YOU HONEY
 I DON'T CARE IF YOU'RE MARRIED
 I WILL DRIVE YOU HOME IN MY ONE-EYED FORD
 WHEE YAH HI, WHEE YAH HI UH YO!

Blackout

Scene 10

The girl injured in the car accident lies, apparently dead, on the stage floor. The young tribespeople show no signs of noticing her body. Night Walker is now more intense.

Photograph by Fred Marvel

NIGHT WALKER

> (*to the young people grouped around him*) This arbor
> cannot be killed. It is strong and powerful. It has lived
> for a very long time. It can be burned and torn apart, but
> its life cannot be taken from it. It draws its life from the
> hearts and souls of the tribe, our people.
>
> There was a time in the journey of our people, when the
> power of the arbor had lost much of its strength.
>
> My grandmother told me the story of this time in our
> people's journey. An old woman from another place
> came into the village. She played with the children, who
> thought she was silly and harmless. She was given a tipi
> to stay in while she visited.
>
> One night, she invited all of the children of the tribe to
> her tipi to tell them stories of the land from where she
> had come.
>
> The children begged her to tell them more; her stories
> were the kind that young people like to hear.
>
> She told them that if they wanted to go to her country
> she would take them. They had to promise her that they
> would do everything that she told them to do. They all
> agreed.
>
> The smoke from her fire became thick. The old woman
> told the children to put their hands into the smoke, and
> the smoke would carry them up through the flap of the
> tipi and out over the night sky to her land. They agreed
> to forget all of the ways of our people while they were on
> the journey.
>
> The children were eager to go to her country. They did
> as the old lady told them to do, and one by one their

figures and voices disappeared from the circle around the fire.

One of the mothers of the tribe went to the tipi to bring her children back to her camp. She cried out when she saw the tipi was empty. The fire was still burning.

The tribespeople became angry. The chiefs had young warriors guard the tipi. A prayer meeting was held. The ceremonial leader sought a vision.

All the tribe crowded around our arbor to hear him tell of what he had seen.

"The children are still in the tipi," the good man told the tribespeople. "The old lady visitor played a trick on them. She promised to take them to her country. But she is the only one who could leave the tipi. The children are safe, they are warm, they are singing and dancing, playing games and telling stories. None of them is quarelling with the others."

"But the tipi is empty, our children are dead, they have been stolen!" the tribespeople cried out. The mothers began to wail.

"They are in the tipi," the old man repeated.

The people did not believe him. They said his vision was wrong. The chiefs pulled in the horses and formed the braves into groups to search for the lost children. The men rode off, leaving only the old people and the women. The wise man stayed under the arbor, praying.

He prayed for many seasons.

The women would not look at him. They wanted to burn the tipi, but he said they would have to kill him if they did. They were afraid to harm the holy man, and he still prayed.

Then the hunting parties began to return to the camp. The men had ridden far in all directions. Their grief was strong for their lost children. They had changed as men.

None of the tribespeople would come to the arbor.

The wise man saw that the fire, which had not stopped burning, had started to go out.

He carried firewood to the tipi and waited outside until the fire had nearly died out. Some of the tribespeople gathered around to watch. The holy man went into the tipi with the firewood and started the fire again. When the flames began to jump from the burning wood, the wise man started to sing. The smoke began rising up through the flap. Many tribespeople were outside the tipi now, watching and talking among themselves.

Suddenly, many voices could be heard singing, the voices of the children. The singing got louder. From outside the tipi the tribespeople could see in now. They saw the figures of their children take shape through the light. The wise man led the singing children out of the tipi and into the arms of their mothers and fathers. The people cried out in happiness.

The wise man led all the people to the arbor. One of the older boys stood to talk before all of the tribe. "We have been inside the tipi," he said. "We could see all of you, but you could not see us. We could not come out until you believed that we were inside. We sang, danced, used the colors." He showed them a pretty breastplate that he had made. "We have changed," he told the tribe. "We are better men and women now."

Night Walker strikes the drum a single hit, then a second one, and the injured girl rises from the stage floor and joins the group.

The tribespeople painted the tipi with beautiful colors and designs. They placed many gifts under the arbor. The arbor once again was covered with the beautiful light of its love for the people.

Rattles, bells, and drum begin, but lowly.

NIGHT WALKER
> (*directly to the young people*) You will pray at the arbor for many seasons. Pray for our tribe to gather beneath it.

YOUNG MAN
> I will always find the willow branches.

YOUNG WOMAN
> And I will place them on the poles.

YOUNG MAN
> I will bring the feathers and the ribbons.

YOUNG WOMAN
> And I will braid them into the branches.

The arbor comes blazingly alight.

PATROL VOICE 1
> Five and 6, you both come through the county road line, block it off 'bout half a mile down from the dance grounds. Don't let any of 'em through, not a car. We'll bottle ever damned one of 'em up in there. Seven, 8, and 9, the four of us'll go in from the main road. All other units in the area'll be in position on 62 and 9. Five and 6, we'll move in when you're sittin' solid. Over.

Drumbeat rises straight up, then stops.

Scene 11

Two young men in the 49 group start a violent pushing and shoving match in the midst of the round dancing. The drumbeat quickens, and the 49 group forms a semicircle around the fighters. The Balladeer appears over the scene and sings as the fight swirls furiously up and down the area.

BALLADEER
(as commentary on the fight)
A HAY HEY A YAH HEY YA HO
A YAH HEY A YAH HEY YA HO
A YAH HEY A HAH HEY YA HO
A YAH HO
A YAH HEY A YAH HEY YO!

A YAH HEY A YAH FIGHT IT OUT!
A YAH HEY A YAH FIGHT IT OUT!
KNOCK HIM OUT! A YAH HEY A YAH HEY YO!

A YAH HEY A YAH CUT HIS HEART!
A YAH HEY A YAH CUT HIS HEART!
A YAH HEY A YAH CUT HIS HEART!
CUT IT OUT! A YAH HEY A YAH HEY YO.

A YAH HEY A YAH TAKE HIS EYE!
A YAH HEY A YAH TAKE HIS EYE!
A YAH HEY A YAH TAKE HIS EYE!
TEAR IT OUT! A YAH HEY A YAH HEY YO.

A YAH HEY A YAH HIT HIM HARD!
A YAH HEY A YAH HIT HIM HARD!
A YAH HEY A YAH KICK HIM HARD
FIGHT ALL NIGHT! A YAH HEY EY YAH HEY EY HO.

A YAH HEY A YAH HEY YA HO

A YAH HEY A YAH HEY YA HO
A YAH HEY A YAH HEY YA HO
A YA HO
A YAH HEY A YAH HEY YO.

Guys from the crowd separate the two fighters, whose girlfriends push through and take their partners. The crowd breaks up.

VOICE OF 49'ER
  (*suddenly, from down the road*) Hi-po's! Cops! Bunch of 'em!
VOICE OF 49'ER
  (*from behind*) Hi-po's! On the back road!
ANOTHER VOICE
  Hi-po's! Comin' in from both directions!

The 49 stops as response develops. Flashes of patrol car spotlights pierce the dark.

PATROL VOICE 1
  (*calmly*) Unit 4. Unit 4. Units 4 and 6 sittin' solid. We got this back road blocked tight. Looks like they're sittin' solid too.
PATROL VOICE 2
  Unit 4 to Units 5 and 6. You read me clear?
PATROL VOICE 1
  Five and 6, we read you clear.
PATROL VOICE 2
  Don't let a single car, repeat, not a single car, get through. They'll sit solid 'til we show 'em we mean business. Group two and three will move in on call.
PATROL VOICE 1
  We read you, Unit 4.
PATROL VOICE 2
  I can see a big gang of 'em right down the road where I'm

sittin'. Looks like about a hunnerd of 'em, kinda' like they're a-walkin' this way. Keep your toplights on. Over.

The 49 group forms a line of defense across the front of the area, facing the police car lights. One of them emerges as a leader. Their voices deepen, as if they are in a kind of trance, but this is to indicate a sudden new strength.

49'ER
Don't come any further!
ANOTHER 49'ER
You're not taking... any... of us!
ANOTHER 49'ER
None of us.

Drumbeat paces the action now. Their attitude of resistance becomes firmer.

PATROL VOICE 1
All right, people, let's break it up! Let's go! Let's get these cars outa here. Ever one of you drivin' one of these cars get out your driver's license. Come on! Let's go! Ever'body else get out your I.D. Let's go!
49'ER
You go!
PATROL VOICE 2
We got you from both ends. Ain't a one of you can get out!
49'ER
We don't want out!
PATROL VOICE 1
(*angry*) I said let's go! Let's move it!

(Brief silence. Drumbeat low.)

PATROL VOICE 2
   We'll move in on you, people. We'll use gas and bring in
   the dogs if we have to.

*The line is strengthened. The sirens blare. Car lights move up
and shine directly in the 49'ers faces. Night Walker, as an
apparition, moves close in.*

49'ER
   You want us. Come and get us!

NIGHT WALKER
   (as a vision) I see a path not walked on. I hear a song not
   yet sung. A fire is burning. I smell the cedar. I see the
   colors strong and shining. There's a circle, round and
   perfect. A beautiful bird is flying.

49'ER
   We'll be here all night!

49'ER
   And all day!

49'ER
   And all night again!

*To a powerful drumbeat and in gymnastic movements, they
form an elaborate barricade with their bodies, allow the image
to strike, then dismantle and form another in the center of the
dance circle. Patrol car lights continue to flash.*

NIGHT WALKER
   A beautiful bird is flying!

*The patrol car lights slowly begin to fade one at a time as the
patrols pull back.*

49'ER
   We'll leave . . . when we're ready to leave!

BALLADEER

 IT'S GOOD WHERE WE'VE BEEN AND WHERE WE'RE
 GOING
 HI YI
 HEY YEY HI YI HI YI HI YA-AY HI YI

 IF YOU GET LOST JUST KEEP ON MOVING
 HI YI
 HEY YEY HI YI HI YI HI YA-AH HI YI

 A BROTHER'S THERE TO WALK BESIDE YOU
 HI YI
 HEY YEY HI YI HI YI HI YA-AY HI YI

 YOUR SISTER'S LOVE IS THERE TO GUIDE YOU
 HI YI
 HEY YEY HI YI HI YI HI YA-AY HI YI

 IT'S GOOD WHERE WE'VE BEEN AND WHERE WE'RE
 GOING
 HI YI
 HEY YEY HI YI HI YI HI YA-AY HI YI.

The change from this scene to the next is paced by the rattles.

Scene 12

*From their defensive positions, the 49 group now turns toward
the center of the circle, where Night Walker is standing in a
shaft of colored light. He is holding a bull-roarer and a rattle.*

NIGHT WALKER

 I am the oldest man of the tribe!
 You have shown me your respect for me.
 You will always have mine.

Photograph by Fred Marvel

Now, at a carefully measured pace, Night Walker creates the effect of a violent storm as he speaks his final incantation. Each time he spins his bull-roarer, one of the young people is propelled to the center of the circle.

NIGHT WALKER
Go!
Go forward!
The tribe needs you.
I go with you.
I am always with you.
We are a tribe!
Of singers.
Of dancers who move with the grace of the bird.
Of people who know color.
Of weavers.
Of good hunters.
We pray.
We are a tribe!
Of people with strong hearts.
Who respect fear
As we make our way.
Who will never kill
Another man's way of living.

The sound of his rattle signals the young people to move out to the edges of the circle. The storm is over, and there is a calm.

NIGHT WALKER
I am the oldest man of the tribe!
I heal my sister's child.
I pray for you.
I sing for you.
I smoke for you.

I give to you these things.
You give them life.

A separate drum begins to beat outside the area. The roadway lights up, and the young people sing as they go off in formation.

YOUNG PEOPLE
    WALKING DOWN THAT POLLEN ROAD
    EVERYTHING IS BEAUTIFUL
    WALKING DOWN THAT POLLEN ROAD
    EVERYTHING IS BEAUTIFUL

    WALKING TO THE EAST
    EVERYTHING IS BEAUTIFUL
    WALKING TO THE NORTH
    EVERYTHING IS BEAUTIFUL
    WALKING TO THE WEST
    EVERYTHING IS BEAUTIFUL
    WALKING TO THE SOUTH
    EVERYTHING IS BEAUTIFUL

    HEY AH NAH HEY NAY
    HEY AH NAH HEY NAY
    HEY AH NAH HEY NAY OH

Night Walker is left alone in the dance circle. After a long pause, during which he faces the audience directly, he turns and walks off as he entered. The chant continues as he leaves, and ends as the lights fade slowly. The arbor is left with a special glow. No curtain.

END

University of Oklahoma Press: Norman and London